1

Introduction to the ASVAB

Taking the ASVAB, like it or not, is not like taking most standardized tests. For one thing, the number of different skills which are being tested is much higher. For another, it is more important than most standardized tests. If you blow it on the SAT, then you can still get into most colleges. It isn't going to affect your future in too big a way. If you blow the ASVAB, on the other hand, it could have a significant effect on your potential future. The ASVAB is what helps recruiters and officials determine your aptitude for certain occupations and specialties within the military and, in fact, what branches you are eligible to join (and whether you can even join at all). Take the test seriously, because it's important. Use this practice question book and any other study materials you have at your disposal in order to prepare for the test and get the most that you can from it. The temptation to skimp on your studying is there, just like with any standardized test, but you simply have to overcome that.

Version Notes – Pen & Pencil vs. Computerized

There are two versions of the ASVAB, which are currently offered: A physical test (pen & pencil) and a computerized version of the test. Both of these versions of the test offer unique challenges and, if possible, you should try to find out which one you will be taking ahead of time. That extra preparation will help give you the best possible chance of succeeding.

The Physical Test – Pen & Pencil

The physical test is much like every other standardized test you have ever taken, but it most closely resembles the SAT or the GRE. Once everyone has arrived and has been seated in the testing room, the administrator will instruct everyone on how the test will be taken. They will then pass out sheets for answers and test booklets. This will include pencils if you have not brought your own (again – you do not need to bring one; they are available to you at the testing center).

The total time for the entire test is somewhere between three and four hours, usually closer to four. You should pay close attention to the instructions given to you by the test administrator and do not advance without being told to. All of the individual aptitudes being tested have their own subtest, which has both a time limit and a specific number of questions on it.

Once each subtest has been finished, you can go back and review the answers that you have chosen, assuming you have enough time left on that test. You are not able to review previous subtests that you have completed, however, and you cannot move on to the next subtest either. The time that you have is only permitted to be used in taking your current subtest or reviewing that subtests answers, and nothing else.

Here is a breakdown of the pen and pencil ASVAB:

Subtest	Time Limit (Minutes)	# Questions
General Science (GS)	11	25
Arithmetic Reasoning (AR)	36	30
Word Knowledge (WK)	11	35
Paragraph Comprehension (PC)	13	15
Mathematics Knowledge (MK)	24	25
Electronics Information (EI)	9	20
Auto and Shop Information (AS)	11	25
Mechanical Comprehension (MC)	19	25
Assembling Objects (AO)	15	25
Totals	149	225

The Computerized Test

The largest difference in the computerized version of the ASVAB (the CAT-ASVAB) is that it is taken on a computer. It is also adaptive. Each time you answer a question, correctly or incorrectly, the test will adapt to your ability level and modify the next questions. This allows the test to be taken in a shorter amount of time than you would have to take on the pencil and paper test.

Prior to beginning the test, an administrator is going to explain how the test is formatted and will give you a brief rundown on how to use a mouse and a keyboard. They will also explain how to answer questions or get help. If you have questions, this is the best time to ask them.

Everyone takes the CAT-ASVAB at a different pace. When you have finished with one subtest, you can immediately move to the next subtest if you want. Time limits are imposed on the individual aptitude tests, but time will rarely expire before you have finished one. The amount of time and remaining questions for each test is displayed on the screen for you. It usually takes about an hour and a half to finish the CAT-ASVAB.

One difference in this and the pen & pencil version of the test that is important to note is that once you have submitted an answer, you cannot review or change it. Another change from the physical version of the test is that auto and shop information have been split into two separate aptitudes, rather than a single subtest.

Here is a breakdown of the computerized ASVAB:

Subtest	Time Limit (Minutes)	# Questions
General Science (GS)	8	16
Arithmetic Reasoning (AR)	39	16
Word Knowledge (WK)	8	16
Paragraph Comprehension (PC)	22	11
Mathematics Knowledge (MK)	20	16
Electronics Information (EI)	8	16
Auto Information (AI)	7	11
Shop Information (SI)	6	11
Mechanical Comprehension (MC)	20	16
Assembling Objects (AO)	16	16
Totals	154	145

The Test Itself – What to Expect

Nothing can ever truly prepare you for the test like just taking it can. You can have all the knowledge in the world about what is on it and how it will go, but for 99.9% of the people taking it, it will be an entirely new experience in an unfamiliar place and, thus, pretty stressful.

The information contained within this section should help ease your mind a bit by explaining some of the nuances involved in the taking of the test.

It should be noted that the version of the ASVAB that you take in high school if you are a member of ROTC, will be a bit different than the version you will take at MEPS. The purpose here is to provide potential career areas for high school students that guidance counselors can use. With that being said, you can still use these scores as your entrance scores for the military if you choose to go that route.

Pre-Exam Considerations

There are a number of things that are going to happen before you take the exam. First, you will need to see a military recruiter (specialized to the branch you are applying to join). The recruiter is going to screen you (and any other applicants) to make sure you will be a good fit and that your candidacy is valid. They will ask about if you have a criminal record, whether you are married, what sort of education you have, basic health-related information, and whether or not you have a history of drug use. These questions, obviously, should be answered as honestly as possible. They may go through a basic physical exam with you as well. Once they have qualified you to move on in the recruitment process, the next step is taking the ASVAB itself.

The test is either going to be administered at an MEPS station or at a METs station, depending on your location. At times, the recruiter that you have been working with will drive you to this station in order for you to take your test. They are not allowed to accompany you inside of the testing room itself, but they are permitted to take you there.

This should be obvious, but DO NOT BE LATE TO THE TEST. If you are late to the test, they will turn you away, and you will have to reschedule your test time. This is not ideal for anyone, so make sure you leave some bumper room in your schedule if you think you might end up cutting it close.

The only thing you need to bring to the test is your social security number (SSN) and a valid photo identification. They will provide you with pencils and test booklets. Calculators are not permitted for use on the test. You may bring your own pencils if you choose, but you will not be required to have one and, again, they will be passed out by the test administrators on test day regardless.

What to Expect During the Exam

During the exam, you can expect a few things. Most of them might seem like common sense, but you should still be aware of them just in case. Here are some of the things you can expect:

- If taking the physical copy of the exam, the times will be a bit longer. You will be given instructions by a proctor, and you will only be able to answer and review the current subtest that you are on. All test materials are provided, and all questions are asked of the proctor.
- If you are taking the computerized version, you cannot go back and review your answers. The time limits are also shorter. This test adapts to your answers, so don't be surprised if the difficulty of the questions changes as you go along through the test.
- The fact that there are time limits on the subtests might stress you out. Be prepared for this and don't let it get to you while you are taking the test.
- You will only be permitted to work on the current subtest you are on, regardless of the type of test you are taking.
- The ASVAB is only administered in English.
- The procedure is going to vary a bit depending on where you are taking the test, so it is never going to be exactly the same.
- If you are late to the test, you will have to leave and reschedule the day of your test.
- You won't be allowed into the testing room if you do not have a valid identification with you.

Post-Exam Considerations

Taking the exam is only part of the process. Once you are done, there are a few things you will still have to do. Get your scores, for one thing. Speaking with your recruiter and letting him or her know how the test went for you is another thing you may want to do.

After the exam, you can expect a few things:

- Your AFQT score will be calculated quickly by the test administrator and provided to your recruiter immediately regardless of which test you take.
- The physical test takes a few days to be scanned, and your score will usually be available afterward.
- If you take the computerized version of the test, your scores will be available to you immediately.
- Do not linger in the test room after the test. Once you are finished, turn it into the proctor and ask to be allowed to leave.
- DO NOT TALK ABOUT THE TEST once it is over. You will be subject to penalties if you write down any of the test questions or talk about the test once you are finished with it. Keep it to yourself and don't spread any information.

Exam Sections

Each section of the ASVAB is meant to test a specific aptitude. There are nine sections in total. Here are the sections covered on the ASVAB, with the possibility that auto/shop might be separated into two disparate sections, depending on whether you take the physical test or the computerized test:

1. General Science
2. Word Knowledge
3. Paragraph Comprehension
4. Mathematics Knowledge
5. Arithmetic Reasoning
6. Electronics Information
7. Auto and Shop Information
8. Mechanical Comprehension
9. Assembling Objects

One thing to note: The subtests are not necessarily going to be in the same order on each test. Do not put too much faith in them being in a specific order and take that into account when you are doing your studies.

What to Expect in the Sections of the ASVAB

Here is a complete series of descriptions for each exam section:

Aptitude	Description
General Science (GS)	This subtest is primarily concerned with the physical sciences and with principles of biology.
Word Knowledge (WK)	Meanings of words, antonyms, synonyms, etc.
Paragraph Comprehension (PC)	Paragraphs of text followed by questions concerned with the content of what you have read.
Mathematics Knowledge (MK)	This is high-school level mathematics, which is going to include both geometry and algebra.
Arithmetic Reasoning (AR)	These are mathematical word problems requiring relatively simple math skills to solve. Logic based, usually.
Electronics Information (EI)	Principles of electronics, basic information about circuits, and terminology.
Auto & Shop Information (AS)	Information about automotive terminology, basic auto and shop skills, and the use of tools.

Mechanical Comprehension (MC)	Principles of basic mechanics and physics.
Assembling Objects (AO)	Orientation of objects in space (physical space – not outer space).

Scoring & Results

There are two different scores that you are going to get when you take the ASVAB. One of them will determine whether or not you are qualified to join the military and which branches you are able to join. The second is the most complete of the two scores. This is the score which is used to help determine your eligibility for various military occupations and specializations. The higher your score, the better your choice of potential specializations will be. It is not possible to get a perfect score, however, so the goal here is to do the best that you can do.

First, you will get what is known as the Armed Forces Qualification Test (AFQT) score. This is the score that will be used to determine whether you are qualified to join specific branches of the military (and whether you can join at all. The AFQT is the composite of the results of the arithmetic reasoning, math knowledge, and both verbal composite (word knowledge and paragraph comprehension) sections of the test.

Here is a list of service branches and the minimum associated AFQT score (these scores could change without notice, as stated in the military and Department of Defense guidelines):

Service Branch	Minimum AFQT Score
Army	31
Navy	35
Marines	31
Air Force	36
Coast Guard	45

The AFQT score is, easily, the most important score of the two for most people. Doing well on this is what will determine whether or not you even have a future in the military. A good analogy would be to consider the AFQT the cake and the other subtests as the icing. If you don't have a good cake, you won't even need the icing.

It should also be noted that most special enlistment programs for individual branches are going to have their own minimum AFQT scores, which often differ significantly from the minimum scores required to join a specific branch:

- **Navy** – Requires anyone with a GED to have a minimum score of 50 for enlistment. Anyone wishing to get in on the college fund or the college repayment program needs also to have a score of 50.
- **Army** – A minimum score of 50 is needed for monetary enlistment bonuses, college repayment programs, and the Army College Fund.
- **Air Force** – A minimum score of 65 is required to enlist in the air force if you have a GED. Their programs are extremely selective, and they want highly skilled candidates.
- **Marine Corps** – The USMC requires a score of 50 on the AFQT for most programs. This includes their enlistment bonuses, the Marine Corps College Fund, and the Navy College Fund.

The second score that you receive will dictate which specializations you are able to enter. This is going to be the results from the other aptitudes which are included on the ASVAB. Unfortunately, the list of specializations that can be entered in the various branches of the military is far too broad and extensive to be listed in this guide. You can, however, find the scores you need and the full list of specializations on the websites for both the military (in general) and on individual branch sites.

If you take the pen & paper version of the test (the physical version), you will get your AFQB score immediately and you will have to wait a few days for the results of the other subtests. If you take the computerized version of the test, you will get your AFQB and your complete ASVAB scores immediately. No questions asked, no need to wait for results. They will be right there waiting for you.

When you get your scores back, you might be expecting one single, easy to understand, score. That is, unfortunately, not the case. You will get a whole bunch of scores. Interpreting these can, at times, be daunting for someone unfamiliar with what they are looking at.

Here are the types of scores you will get back:

- **Standard score** – This is the method that your subtests will be reported back to you. They are based on a standard distribution that has a mean of 50 and usually has a standard deviation of 10. This is NOT a 1-100 grading system like you would have seen in school, so do not confuse it with that.

- **Raw score** – This is the total of the number of points you have gotten on the subtests. Questions are weighted differently. These scores are used to help calculate the other scores, but raw scores will not usually be shown on your results card.
- **Percentile score** – These have a range of 1-99 and help to compare your scores with the "normal" group. It shows what percentile of test takers you are in. The higher your score here, the better you did, relatively speaking.
- **Composite score** – Individually calculated scores for each individual branch of the military. They all have their own way of handling this.

The calculation of the AFQT score itself follows a relatively simple procedure:

- First the value of your Paragraph Comprehension score is added to your Word Knowledge score.
- Next, the resulting number will be converted to a scaled score (your verbal expression score) which has a range between 20 and 62.
- Next you will double that verbal expression score and add your Mathematics Knowledge and Arithmetic Reasoning scores to it. This will give you your raw score.
- Finally, that score is converted to a percentile score which compares the results of your test with other individuals who have taken the test.

Your percentile score is going to be used to help determine your trainability for each individual branch. The following table should help you to determine where you stand:

Percentile Score	Trainability	Category
93-100	Outstanding	I
65-92	Excellent	II
50-64	Above average	III A
31-49	Average	III B
21-30	Below average	IV A
16-20	Markedly below average	IV B
10-15	Poor	IV C
0-9	Not trainable	V

Only four percent of applicants from category IV can be taken into the military. No applicants from category V may be taken. These figures come from the Department of Defense.

All ASVAB test scores are valid for a period of two years. If you do not qualify with your current test scores, you are allowed to retest, as dictated by each individual branch:

- **Air Force** – No retesting is allowed for delayed entry programs. If you have no job preference but have qualified scores otherwise, you may retest. You can retest if the line scores of your subtests limit the matching ability of currently available jobs. You may retest to improve your scores, but the recruiting flight chief has to interview you in person to give approval prior to any retesting.
- **Army** – You may retest if your scores have expired, if you fail to meet the AFQT requirements, or if extenuating circumstances occur (having to leave the test due to an emergency, etc.).
- **Marine Corps** – Retests can be given once the previous test scores have expired and at the discretion of recruiters. They cannot be requested only on the basis that the scores were too low for enlistment programs.
- **Navy** – If your scores have expired, the test can be retaken. The test can also be retaken if your scores are too low to enlist.
- **Coast Guard** – Tests can be retaken after six months in order to raise scores to qualify for certain enlistment options. The recruiters may also authorize retests after 30 days at their discretion.

General Test Tips

Even the simplest test will have some tips which are universal. In this section, tips are included to help you on the ASVAB in a generalized way, regardless of which type of test you are taking or which aptitude test you are currently on. In fact, most of these tips will help you on any kind of standardized test that might take, no matter what subject the test is on (MCAT, SAT, GRE, ASVAB, LSAT, etc.).

Here are some tips to utilize before the test:

- Begin preparing for your test as early as you possibly can. If you do not feel as though you are quite ready for it, then do not put pressure on yourself to take it early. With regard to the ASVAB, recruiters may, at times, try to railroad you into taking the test as quickly as possible (sometimes within a couple of days of speaking with them). If you feel like you are not ready, schedule the test for a later date.
- Plan very carefully ahead of time and use your time wisely. Do not waste time or procrastinate on your studying.

- Study at the same general time every day. Don't let yourself become sidetracked doing other things when you should be spending the time studying.
- Make sure you study in a well-lit and quiet area. Somewhere comfortable. Avoid distractions if possible. This is a great time to utilize a public library.
- Remember to get a good night sleep and eat well prior to the test. Remember to relax and do not allow yourself to become too stressed out about what is going on in your life. Don't eat a carb heavy meal the morning of the test, however, because it might make you tired during the test and affect your ability to concentrate.
- When you are taking practice tests, you will want to make sure that you time yourself in the same way that you will be timed on the real test. This will give you the greatest feel for how the test will actually be administered. Many people who neglect to do this wind up finding themselves short on time when the test is actually being taken.
- Avoid drinking lots of fluid (water or otherwise) prior to the test. You could wind up wasting a lot of the time during your test simply going to the bathroom. Don't make that mistake.
- Make sure you bring supplies *just in case*. While you will be given pencils and paper, it would pay to bring pencils, erasers, pens, and scratch paper just in case. You can never be too careful. Make sure you have your contacts, a backup set, and glasses if you need them as well.
- A watch might help you keep track of time during the physical version of the test (in case there is not a clock in the room). It will pay to invest in a watch if you don't already have one just to be extra careful.

Here are a few tips for making the most of your study materials and practice sessions ahead of time:

- Make sure you study the information *about* the test just as much as you study what is *on* the test. This means the types of questions you might face, the format of the test, the length of time you have for each test section, etc.
- Take adequate time to prepare by taking a practice test at regular intervals throughout your study. This will let you find your weak points so that you can narrowly focus on them. Besides the obvious, this will also alert you to weak points in areas that take longer amounts of time to study, such as vocabulary, paragraph comprehension, and grammar.

- Do not spend too much time on your strong points. Review them, yes, but do not spend an inordinate amount of time going over materials that you already have a firm grasp on.

- Analyze why you missed questions on the practice test. Was it because you second guessed yourself? Was it because you just didn't know how to answer the question? Remember: the more information you have, the better.

- Do not try to memorize the answers to questions. Figure out what the question is about and study it. Specific questions are not as important as having a firm grasp of the concepts being tested.

- Do not try to memorize everything in this guide (or any guide) in a small time window. It simply won't work. In fact, it will probably undermine the work that you are trying to accomplish.

- Generalize the types of thinking that you will have to use during each aptitude test you will take.

- Make sure you spend time on every part of the guide during your studies. All of them are unique, and all of them will help.

- Multiple short study sessions are better than single long study sessions.

Here are some strategies you can use to help you narrow down answers:

- Break down the amount of time that you actually have to spend on individual questions. This can be found by dividing the test time by the number of questions.

- Make sure you read through every single answer prior to marking anything. You have to keep in mind that many tests want you to select the "best" answer, meaning more than one might be correct, but one of them is "more" correct than the others. Do not make any snap judgments about a particular answer without reading the others, because more than one might be technically correct.

- Use clues within the question to help you select the answer and make an educated guess.

- Run through the test questions very quickly to get the easy ones out of the way first (for the pen and paper version, at least). That way you can determine which questions you will need to spend more time on.

- If all else fails, go with your gut. People will often second-guess themselves and end up marking the wrong answer. If you lean toward a certain answer right from the start, then go with it.

14

- Eliminate any answers that you can right from the start. On multiple choice tests, two or sometimes three answers will often be obviously wrong. Cross through them or ignore them so that you do not waste valuable time.
- Always read the full directions before going to try and select answers. This is shockingly important, and it is something that many individuals, for whatever reason, do not do. Big mistake.

Finally, there is one other thing you need to remember: FOLLOW THE RULES DURING THE TEST. Don't do anything that might be misconstrued as cheating. Don't take to anyone. Avoid shifting your eyes around to others. Only ask questions to the test administrator. Do not copy down any questions to your papers. If you finish a section early (on the physical version of the test), review your answers. Do not sneak looks at material not being covered yet.

Practice Exams

The following practice exams will take you through all of the individual sections of the ASVAB subtest by subtest. Consult the introductory section of this book and time yourself according to the time limits that have been laid out there.

By completing this practice test, you will have a good idea of where you stand when it comes to the actual ASVAB. If you don't do well, do not beat yourself up. Studying for the ASVAB takes a significant amount of time and effort, and every step that you take toward your goal is another brick on the road to success.

GENERAL SCIENCE

1. What is the basic unit of volume in the metric system?
    a. meter
    b. milliliter
    c. liter
    d. gram

2. What is the field of geology primarily concerned with?
    a. the Earth
    b. volcanos
    c. the sky
    d. the moon

3. There are two primarily building blocks which are used by plants during photosynthesis in order to make sugars (primarily glucose). What are they?
    a. water and carbon dioxide
    b. dirt and air
    c. nitrogen and carbon
    d. water and oxygen

4. What is the fundamental biological unit that is used in order to build protein structures?
    a. nucleic acids
    b. amino acids
    c. elements
    d. Water

5. What is chemistry?
    a. study of chemical elements
    b. study of the earth
    c. study of the planets
    d. the study of life

6. What is the organ of the human body which helps to pump blood throughout the circulatory system?

    a. lungs
    b. heart
    c. hemoglobin
    d. brain

7. In 1 inch, there are 2.54 centimeters. In 1 foot, there are 12 inches. How many centimeters are there in 1 foot?

    a. 30.48
    b. 10.43
    c. 12
    d. 24.5

8. The outermost part of a cell is known as the plasma membrane. What is the plasma membrane called in plants and bacteria (and some fungi)?

    a. plasma membrane
    b. permeable membrane
    c. cell wall
    d. mosaic membrane

9. What is one method to convert the Celsius scale to the Fahrenheit scale?

    a. $C = F+32$
    b. $C = 32 + (9/5) F$
    c. $F = 32 + C(5/9)$
    d. $C = 95 * F$

10. Which organ is the location at which circulating blood is oxygenated in order to carry oxygen to the tissues of the body?

    a. brain
    b. heart
    c. lungs
    d. skin

11. Which kind of subatomic particle is found outside of the nucleus (and carries a negative charge)?

    a. electronino

    b. neutron

    c. proton

    d. electron

12. What is absolute zero?

    a. 0 Celsius

    b. 0 Kelvin

    c. -32 Celsius

    d. 0 Fahrenheit

13. The process of cell division which results in two daughter cells with the same number of chromosomes as the parent cell is _____.

    a. mitosis

    b. division

    c. meiosis

    d. sex

14. Which subatomic particle is used to determine the atomic number of an element?

    a. neutron

    b. proton

    c. neutrino

    d. electron

15. What is the term that is primarily used for a gene which will be expressed even when a different allele is present?

    a. pragmatic

    b. recessive

    c. dominant

    d. denim

16. _____ is the process through which cells convert the nutrients that they received into ATP.
    a. cellular respiration
    b. diffusion
    c. permeability
    d. nuclear splitting

17. What is the highest (broadest) level of classification in biology?
    a. phylum
    b. species
    c. class
    d. kingdom

18. What is the first element on the periodic table?
    a. plutonium
    b. iron
    c. hydrogen
    d. helium

19. What color of light is *not* used by the leaves of most plants?
    a. red
    b. blue
    c. violet
    d. green

20. What is the definition of "force"?
    a. weight due to gravity
    b. the color of an object
    c. speed across a distance
    d. interaction resulting in a change of motion

21. What type of energy is used by plants during the process of photosynthesis in order to assist in making sugar?
    a. moonlight
    b. sunlight
    c. electricity
    d. friction

22. What is the study of physics concerned with?
    a. matter and its motion
    b. chemical substances
    c. life processes
    d. telekinesis

23. _____ is a term which is used to describe the changes in organisms over a period of time in terms of their traits and genes.
    a. chemistry
    b. biology
    c. evolution
    d. astronomy

24. What is the basic unit of distance in the metric system?
    a. liter
    b. meter
    c. gram
    d. centimeter

25. What is genetic drift?
    a. when a group of individuals leaves a large population and becomes genetically different over time
    b. when genes float through the bloodstream
    c. when seeds float on air currents
    d. when biological "rafts" carry cells to new locations

ARITHMETIC REASONING

1. If the total sum of the ages of William, Scott, and Jim is 80 years, then what was the sum of their ages five years ago?
    a. 75 years
    b. 65 years
    c. 50 years
    d. 69 years

2. A company is organizing a party for one of their employees who is retiring. $1/5^{th}$ of the women in the office decided to attend along with $1/8^{th}$ of the men. What is the fraction of the total number of employees who attended the retirement party?
    a. 5/13
    b. 26/80
    c. Not enough information
    d. None of these answers

3. Some friends are going to go to a potluck. Everyone has decided to spend a total sum of $96 on the food they are bringing. Four of the people who were supposed to attend did not show. Because of their absence, everyone had to kick in an extra $4 to make up the difference in food cost. How many people attended the potluck total?
    a. 96
    b. 14
    c. 20
    d. 8

4. Bags of apples cost $7 a piece. Bags of pears cost $5 a piece. Jim goes to the store and spends a total of $38. How many bags of pears did he buy?
    a. 1
    b. 2
    c. 3
    d. 4

5. Select the next 4 numbers in the following series: (2, 4, 6, 8...)
    a. 10, 12, 14, 16
    b. 9, 10, 11, 12
    c. 1, 3, 5, 7
    d. 12, 14, 16, 18

6. John operates a small saw mill. Out of the workers at the mill, one-fourth of them are female, and one-eighth of them are from out of town. What proportion of the mill workers would you expect to be both female and from out of town?
    a. 1/4
    b. 1/5
    c. 1/8
    d. 1/40

7. There is a clinic that operates in the town, employing 214 total employees. Out of those 214, 63 of them are male. What percentage of the employees of the hospital are male, rounded to the nearest percent?
    a. 10%
    b. 30%
    c. 29.9%
    d. 28.8%

8. What is the product of 87 and 92, rounded to the nearest ten?
    a. 8,004
    b. 8,000
    c. 8,800
    d. 7,800

9. Patients who are severely burned need to have treatment quickly. Once 1 hour has passed, the chance that the patient will survive begins to drop. It drops at a rate of around 12% for every hour after the first that passes. If the individual does not get treatment for 6 hours, what is their chance of survival?
   a. 72%
   b. 60%
   c. 40%
   d. 28%

10. John is trying to figure out what his average test grade is for the semester. He knows that the lowest grade he received on a test will be dropped and will not be used to figure out the average. His scores are 64, 21, 76, 80, and 85. What is his average?
    a. 76.25%
    b. 76%
    c. 65%
    d. 65.2%

11. Jane earns $15 per hour babysitting. If she starts out with $275 in her bank account, which of the following equations represents how many hours will she have to babysit for her account to reach $400?
    a. -400=15h-275
    b. 400=15/h+275
    c. 400=15h
    d. 400=15h+275

12. If a map has a scale of 1/8 of an inch equaling 5 miles and the map is 12 inches, how many miles across does the map cover?
    a. 400
    b. 1200
    c. 4800
    d. 480

13. In a pack of 100 dogs, 86% of them are female. How many dogs is female?
    a. 8
    b. 86
    c. 860
    d. 8.6

14. A rest home in the local area has 56 males and 93 females. Out of the residents, what is the percentage of male residents?
    a. 56%
    b. 37%
    c. 37.5%
    d. 149

15. There is a drug that is being tested which works on cluster headaches, a specific type of a migraine. The drug has a 25% rate of success in treating these headaches. Around 8% of migraines are cluster headaches. What percent of migraines will this drug work on?
    a. 25%
    b. 8%
    c. 22%
    d. 2%

16. At a bake sale, muffins are priced at $1.50 each and cookies are priced at $1 for two. If 11 muffins were sold, and the total money earned was $29.50, how many cookies were sold?
    a. 12
    b. 13
    c. 23
    d. 26

17. The post office is having trouble figuring out their staffing. They need to have one person to deliver mail for every 183 houses in the town. The town has 2,984 houses. How many mail carriers will have to be hired?

    a. 16.3
    b. 17
    c. 18
    d. 20

18. You go to the local electronics store to buy some movies. Each movie costs $9.95. You buy seven movies. How much change will you receive back if you pay with two $50 bills?

    a. $30.05
    b. $30
    c. $69.95
    d. none of the above

19. A restaurant employs servers, hosts, and managers in a ratio of 9:2:1. If there are 36 total employees, how many hosts are there?

    a. 4
    b. 3
    c. 6
    d. 8

20. Two people are racing, A and B. A finishes the race with a time of 3.2 minutes. B finishes the race with a time of 235 seconds. What is the difference in their times?

    a. 34 seconds
    b. 43 minutes
    c. 43 seconds
    d. 25% of a minute

21. You go to the local grocery store to buy some bottles of water. The water comes in packs of 6. Each pack of 6 costs $12. You need to pick up 18 sodas total. What will your price be?

    a. $26
    b. $36
    c. $12
    d. $18

22. In a neighborhood, 2/5 of the houses are painted yellow. If there are 24 houses that are not painted yellow, how many yellow houses are in the neighborhood?

    a. 16
    b. 9.6
    c. 24
    d. 40

23. Mitch wants to buy a home. The home costs $100,000 with an annual percentage rate (only on the $100,000) of 7%. How much will he owe after 5 years?

    a. $135,000
    b. $13,500
    c. $100,000
    d. $35,000

24. 7 is what percent of 60?

    a. 11.67%
    b. 4.20%
    c. 8.57%
    d. 10.11%

25. Simplify the expression $[5(x^2)]^{10}$.

    a. $[5x]^{20}$
    b. $[5x]^{12}$
    c. $5x^{(-8)}$
    d. $[50x]^2$

26. A man is three times the age of his son. He was four times the age of his son five years ago. How old is the son?
    a. 20
    b. 12
    c. 18
    d. 15

27. Rahim is three times the age of Paul, who is 12. How old is Rahim?
    a. 36
    b. 15
    c. 9
    d. 42

28. How many days does it take 4 cats to kill 4 mice? 100 cats are able to kill 100 mice in a period of 100 days.
    a. 100 days
    b. 4 days
    c. 10 days
    d. 1 day

29. Josh, Alex, and Drake have ages that total to 75 years. What was that total two years ago?
    a. 69 years
    b. 81 years
    c. 6 years
    d. 25 years

30. Jim is working on a project. He is completing 12% of the work per hour. How many hours will it take him to finish the project to completion (rounded to the nearest hour)?
    a. 8 hours
    b. 8.3 hours
    c. 9 hours
    d. 0.7 hours

WORD KNOWLEDGE

1. _____ is a word that is a synonym of hardship.
    a. ease
    b. corrosive
    c. care
    d. hardship

2. What is the definition of the word **grudging?**
    a. rocky
    b. smoothing
    c. not generous
    d. close

3. The parents were afraid the children were going to **mar** the living room furniture.
    a. damage
    b. fix
    c. move
    d. climb on

4. What is a **scabbard**?
    a. a painting
    b. the hook to hang a clock
    c. an Arabic boat
    d. a sheath used for a sword or dagger

5. "She **upbraided** her husband when he came in with mud on his boots." **Upbraid** most closely means:
    a. scold
    b. hug
    c. love
    d. hate

6. **Warble** means:
    a. ogle
    b. quaver
    c. cross
    d. drown

7. Which of the following is a possible definition of the word **minute**?
    a. an opinion
    b. a stain
    c. immeasurably small
    d. very large

8. The French signed the peace **accord** to end the war.
    a. an argument
    b. a treaty
    c. a piece of paper
    d. a scroll

9. Which of the following words is most closely an antonym of **evident**?
    a. clear
    b. angry
    c. hidden
    d. in the air

10. What does **fraught** mean?
    a. cute
    b. fast
    c. worried
    d. rare

11. The man **intended** to go to work, but he ended up at the movies instead.
    a. planned
    b. did not want
    c. loved
    d. hated

12. **Conceit** means:
   a. a type of jacket
   b. slowly
   c. quickly
   d. arrogant

13. The _____ student was smart enough to learn, but did not want to, and he was put into the corner to think about what he had done.
   a. apt
   b. refractory
   c. victorious
   d. foolish

14. Which of the following words most closely matches the definition of the word equable?
   a. awesome
   b. dead
   c. rotten
   d. temperate

15. If someone is devoted to the care of sheep or some sort of cattle, you might describe their life as:
   a. farm-heavy
   b. boring
   c. pastoral
   d. leaden

16. The crying woman in the field had received the news in a way unintended by the messenger, and she experienced clear _____, bordering on alarm.
   a. disapprobation
   b. anger
   c. happiness
   d. joy

17. If you were to omit or suppress part of a word or a sentence, you have made an:

    a. error

    b. ellipsis

    c. choice

    d. mistake

18. **Pusillanimous** most closely means:

    a. loving

    b. cowardly

    c. strong

    d. putrid

19. What is a **yeoman**?

    a. the farmer who works land that he owns

    b. slave

    c. market

    d. yak owner

20. What is a **precept**?

    a. A teacher

    b. A representative

    c. Someone who came first

    d. A doctrine being taught

21. The current state of surveillance in the United States is something which is being maintained by a _____ of corporate interests and government agencies.

    a. anger

    b. friendship

    c. nexus

    d. trickery

22. A type of legislation which is used to help ingratiate representatives with the constituents that they have under them is called:
    a. bacon grease
    b. pork barrel
    c. animal bucket
    d. filibuster

23. She **ensconced** herself in the lounge chair.
    a. fix firmly
    b. sleep
    c. fall
    d. feel sick

24. What is a synonym of **punctually**?
    a. late
    b. duly
    c. too fast
    d. punctured

25. What is a **vicissitude**?
    a. a type of intestinal disorder
    b. many-legged insect
    c. a change in circumstance
    d. a strong wind

26. **Pendulous** is a word which means ____.
    a. strong
    b. tough
    c. stalwart
    d. drooping

27. John was a **bibliophile**, choosing to spend the majority of his time in libraries.
    a. loved books
    b. hated books
    c. loved libraries
    d. loves to read

28. What is a **nicety**?
    a. mean word
    b. nuance
    c. open statement
    d. proxy

29. If someone is undergoing **privation**, they are:
    a. celebrities
    b. private people
    c. rich
    d. lacking necessities

30. **Superannuated** is a term that means:
    a. brand new
    b. old
    c. born last year
    d. tough

31. Any fact which has been well established throughout the course of history cannot be **gainsaid** easily.
    a. loved
    b. written about
    c. taken exception to
    d. accepted

32. What does it mean to **execrate**?
    a. to love unconditionally
    b. to run away quickly
    c. to defecate
    d. to curse or despise

33. What is one possible definition of the word **conceit**?
    a. not-permitted
    b. tight
    c. turn of phrase
    d. grouped closely

34. What is the term for a closed meeting of members of the same political party?
    a. election
    b. caucus
    c. meeting
    d. vote

35. What does I it mean if you yell in a **stentorian** way?
    a. quietly
    b. with a booming voice
    c. silently
    d. with anger

PARAGRAPH COMPREHENSION

Prompt 1:

Young Conrad's birthday was fixed for his espousals. The company was assembled in the chapel of the Castle, and everything ready for beginning the divine office, when Conrad himself was missing. Manfred, impatient of the least delay, and who had not observed his son retire, despatched one of his attendants to summon the young Prince. The servant, who had not stayed long enough to have crossed the court to Conrad's apartment, came running back breathless, in a frantic manner, his eyes staring, and foaming at the month. He said nothing, but pointed to the court.

The Castle of Otranto by Horace Walpole

1. What is the general mood of this passage?
   a. Happy
   b. Depressing
   c. Frantic
   d. Hopeful

2. On which day was Conrad to be married?
   a. The birthday of his wife.
   b. His own birthday.
   c. His father's birthday.
   d. The day after his birthday/

Prompt 2:

In the past, many cars were a manual transmission. Today, however, cars have shifted over to automatic transmission (for the most part). Shifting gears in a manual, however, is an important skill to learn if you plan to hit the road. Simply depress the clutch and then shift with the shifting lever to get the right gear. Then release the clutch and apply pressure to the gas at the same time.

3. Why have cars shifted from
   a. because manuals no longer work
   b. manuals are too complex
   c. to lower costs
   d. not enough information

4. What is the second step in shifting gears in a manual transmission?
    a. press the gas
    b. press the clutch
    c. move the shifting lever
    d. press the brake

5. What kind of transmission are most modern cars?
    a. automatic
    b. manual
    c. shifting
    d. auto gear

Prompt 3:

These visions faded when I perused, for the first time, those poets whose effusions entranced my soul and lifted it to heaven. I also became a poet and for one year lived in a paradise of my own creation; I imagined that I also might obtain a niche in the temple where the names of Homer and Shakespeare are consecrated. You are well acquainted with my failure and how heavily I bore the disappointment. But just at that time I inherited the fortune of my cousin, and my thoughts were turned into the channel of their earlier bent.

Frankenstein by Mary Shelley

6. Why did the narrator stop having "visions"?
    a. he discovered poetry
    b. he died
    c. he went to heaven
    d. his soul was lost

7. Where did the narrator live after becoming a poet?
    a. his house
    b. a paradise of his own creation
    c. a temple
    d. none of the above

Prompt 4:

Jim was going to the store to buy apples when he was sidetracked. Sally had been following him the entire time and finally decided to call out. Jim has broken up with her for a reason, and it was ridiculous to think she was still trying to get his attention.

8. Why might Jim not be happy to see Sally?
    a. he is too busy to talk to her
    b. she hates apples
    c. they broke up
    d. she hates him

Prompt 5:

The House of Representatives shall be composed of Members chosen every second Year by the People of the several States, and the Electors in each State shall have the Qualifications requisite for Electors of the most numerous Branch of the State Legislature.

The United States Constitution

9. How often are the members of the House of Representatives elected?
    a. every 4 years
    b. every 3 years
    c. every year
    d. every 2 years

Prompt 6:

When in the Course of human events, it becomes necessary for one people to dissolve the political bands which have connected them with another, and to assume among the powers of the earth, the separate and equal station to which the Laws of Nature and of Nature's God entitle them, a decent respect to the opinions of mankind requires that they should declare the causes which impel them to the separation.

The Declaration of Independence

10. What is this prompt introducing?
    a. the reasons for a separation
    b. reasons to stay together
    c. a revolution
    d. human history

11. Which of the following might mean the same as "dissolve political bands"?
    a. make a treaty
    b. get rid of the government
    c. abolish slavery
    d. move away

Prompt 7:

Vampires are known to be wary of men who have, on their person, garlic, crosses, holy water, or bibles. They tend to steer clear of these men, as they see them as dangerous to their continued existence.

12. Which of the following do vampires avoid?
    a. garlic
    b. holy water
    c. crosses
    d. all of the above

Prompt 8:

No Senator or Representative shall, during the Time for which he was elected, be appointed to any civil Office under the Authority of the United States, which shall have been created, or the Emoluments whereof shall have been encreased during such time; and no Person holding any Office under the United States, shall be a Member of either House during his Continuance in Office.

The United States Constitution

13. What is this meant to state?
    a. Representatives cannot create job for themselves and give themselves those jobs
    b. Representatives cannot be paid
    c. Representatives cannot be civil servants
    d. Representatives must quit their jobs

Prompt 9:

Today was not a good day. It all started with the rain in the morning. The windows were down on the car, so the seats got all wet. Then the call from Juliet, and the breakup. After that, I lost my job. Today was not a good day at all.

14. What was the last sign that "today was not a good day?
    a. rain
    b. car seat
    c. call from Juliet
    d. lost job

Prompt 10:

When Dr. Van Helsing and Dr. Seward had come back from seeing poor Renfield, we went gravely into what was to be done. First, Dr. Seward told us that when he and Dr. Van Helsing had gone down to the room below they had found Renfield lying on the floor, all in a heap. His face was all bruised and crushed in, and the bones of the neck were broken.

Dracula by Bram Stoker

15. What does the narrator mean by "went gravely into what was to be done"?
    a. kill each other
    b. go to a grave
    c. dig a grave
    d. make a plan

MATHEMATICS KNOWLEDGE

1. A woman's dinner bill comes to $48.30. If she adds a 20% tip, what will she pay in total?
   a. $9.66
   b. $38.64
   c. $68.30
   d. $57.96

2. Evaluate the expression $\frac{x^2-2y}{y}$ when $x = 20$ and $y = \frac{x}{2}$.
   a. 0
   b. 38
   c. 36
   d. 19

3. Adam is painting the outside of a 4-walled shed. The shed is 5 feet wide, 4 feet deep, and 7 feet high. How much paint will Adam need?
   a. 126 ft^2
   b. 140 ft^3
   c. 63 ft^2
   d. 46 feet

4. Liz is installing a tile backsplash. If each tile is an equilateral triangle with sides that measure 6 centimeters in length, how many tiles does she need to cover an area of 1800 square centimeters?
   a. 36 tiles
   b. 100 tiles
   c. 50 tiles
   d. 300 tiles

5. $2.31 * 10^2 =$
   a. 23.1
   b. 231
   c. 2310
   d. 23100

6. If $f(x) = |x - 28|$, evaluate $f(-12)$.

   a. -16

   b. 40

   c. 16

   d. -40

7. $10^8 / 10^3 =$

   e. 10^5

   f. 10^6

   g. 10^{11}

   h. 10^{10}

8. What is 15% of 986?

   i. 146.9

   j. 98.6

   k. 9.86

   l. 147.9

9. A circular swimming pool has a circumference of 49 feet. What is the diameter of the pool?

   a. 15.6 feet

   b. 12.3 feet

   c. 7.8 feet

   d. 17.8 feet

10. 50% of 94 is:

    m. 42

    n. 52

    o. 45

    p. 47

11. If ∡A measures 57°, find ∡G.

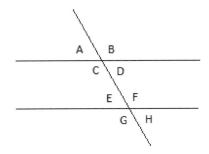

  a. 57°
  b. 147°
  c. 123°
  d. 33°

12. The table below shows the number of hours worked by employees during the week.
   What is the median number of hours worked per week by the employees?

Employee	Suzanne	Joe	Mark	Ellen	Jill	Rob	Nicole	Deb
Hours worked per week	42	38	25	50	45	46	17	41

  a. 38
  b. 41
  c. 42
  d. 41.5

13. Multiply the following terms: $(11xy)(2x^2y)$
  a. $13xy + x$
  b. $22x^3y^2$
  c. $44x^3y^3$
  d. $22xy^2 + 2x^2$

14. y = 2x − 5. x = 10. What is y?
  q. 10
  r. 20
  s. 15
  t. 5

15. x=2, y = -3, z = 4. Solve x+y*z

     u.   -4

     v.   10

     w. -12

     x.   -10

16. Factor the expression $64 - 100x^2$.

     a. $(8 + 10x)(8 - 10x)$

     b. $(8 + 10x)^2$

     c. $(8 - 10x)^2$

     d. $(8 + 10x)(8x + 10)$

17. Which expression would you solve first in the following: (9+9) x 987 + 4^6

     a. 4^6

     b. (9+9)

     c. 9 X 987

     d. 987 + 4

18. Solve for y: $10y - 8 - 2y = 4y - 22 + 5y$

     a. $y = -4\frac{2}{3}$

     b. $y = 14$

     c. $y = 30$

     d. $y = -30$

19. Solve for x: $(2x + 6)(3x - 15) = 0$

     a. $x = -5,3$

     b. $x = -3,5$

     c. $x = -2, -3$

     d. $x = -6,15$

20. Round 0.1938562 to the nearest tenth.

    y. 0.0

    z. 0.2

    aa. 0.19

    bb. 0.194

21. Points B and C are on a circle, and a chord is formed by line segment $\overline{BC}$. If the distance from the center of the circle to point B is 10 centimeters, and the distance from the center of the circle to the center of line segment $\overline{BC}$ is 8 centimeters, what is the length of line segment $\overline{BC}$?

    a. 6 centimeters

    b. 4 centimeters

    c. 12 centimeters

    d. 14 centimeters

22. If $f(x) = 3^x - 2$, evaluate $f(5)$.

    a. 27

    b. 243

    c. 241

    d. 13

23. If a spherical water balloon is filled with 113 milliliters of water, what is the approximate radius of the balloon? (Note: The volume, V, of a sphere with radius r is found using the equation $V = \frac{4}{3}\pi r^3$.)

    a. 4.0 centimeters

    b. 3.0 centimeters

    c. 3.6 centimeters

    d. 3.3 centimeters

24. Simplify 13/26 into a decimal.

    a. 0.13

    b. 0.16

    c. 0.5

    d. 0.25

25. Factor the expression $100x^2+25x$.

    a. $100x(x+25x)$

    b. $25(4x+x)$

    c. $25x(4x+1)$

    d. $25(4x^2+x)$

ELECTRONICS INFORMATION

1. What does the following image represent?

    a. voltage meter

    b. RAM

    c. computer

    d. integrated circuit

2. An ohm is used to measure what?

    a. force

    b. resistance

    c. power

    d. voltage

3. Which of the following devices would be able to turn electrical energy into sound waves?

    a. speaker

    b. wires

    c. tuning fork

    d. fire

4. What would a squiggly line in a circuit diagram represent?

    a. resistor

    b. conductor

    c. wire

    d. ground line

5. Which of the following is typically used to measure electrical energy?

    a. current

    b. volts

    c. kilowatt-hours

    d. watt-ohms

6. The _____ is the part of a given circuit which carries no voltage. Fill in the blank.

    a. fuse

    b. wire

    c. load

    d. ground

7. What force can be created by a current of electricity moving through a wire?

    a. magnetic force

    b. friction

    c. gravity

    d. resistance

8. What will be the most common result of a short circuit?
    a. light bulbs will explode
    b. a circuit breaker will trip
    c. the wire will cool down very quickly
    d. none of the above

9. The word "circuit" is commonly used in electronics. What is it?
    a. electricity
    b. a computer chip
    c. the path a current follows
    d. how voltage moves

10. The movement of which subatomic particle is responsible for electricity?
    a. protons
    b. electrons
    c. neutrons
    d. nuclei

11. When electrons move between two points, what is being created?
    a. pressure
    b. voltmeter
    c. force
    d. current

12. If the electrical potential is high at one end of a wire and low at the other, what will happen?
    a. current will flow to the low end
    b. current will flow to the high end
    c. the current will escape
    d. pressure will build, causing a fire

13. Changing AC to DC requires the use of a...
    a. transformer
    b. current switcher
    c. current manufacturing plant
    d. breaker box

14. Which one of these would be the least effective as a conductor?
    a. lead
    b. wood
    c. water
    d. copper

15. When a current goes over a certain value, a _____ can be installed which will melt and break the circuit. Fill in the blank.
    a. wire breaker
    b. breaker
    c. fuse
    d. current stopper

16. What is the definition of voltage?
    a. electricity moving
    b. electric tension
    c. electric kinetic energy
    d. electric pressure

17. Which of the following is used to measure voltage?
    a. voltage test unit
    b. voltage regulator
    c. voltmeter
    d. voltmeter

18. One joule per coulomb is also known as:

    a. 1 volt

    b. 1 ohm

    c. 1 resistor

    d. 1 potential

19. What makes integrated circuits possible?

    a. semiconductors

    b. metal

    c. conductors

    d. gold leaf

20. What common household device might you find a filament?

    a. integrated circuit

    b. microwave

    c. lamp

    d. computer

AUTO & SHOP INFORMATION

1. Four stroke engine cycles work in specific ways. They follow the intake - _____ - power – exhaust cycles. What is the part of the cycle that belongs in the blank space in this four-stroke engine cycle?
   a. compression
   b. decompression
   c. combustion
   d. power intake

2. If you were going to use a bolt to fasten two things together, what would you have to use to tighten the connection?
   a. screw
   b. drill bit
   c. ratchet
   d. nut

3. What is one of the possible reasons that a vehicle might have a better fuel efficiency rating?
   a. the gas costs less
   b. the gas tank is larger
   c. the vehicle costs less
   d. the vehicle is lighter

4. What would you use a plane for?
   a. to remove large portions of material
   b. to remove small bits of material, smoothing
   c. to roughen a surface
   d. to make things fit tighter

5. If someone told you that their vehicle had an inline 6 for the engine, what would they be indicating?
   a. the vehicle is lined up from all 6 directions
   b. there are 6 cylinders
   c. the engine is 6 feet long, in a single line
   d. the gas tank is in line with the vehicle and holds 6 gallons

6. What voltage would you expect to find in a typical commercial car battery sold in your local auto parts store?
    a. 6 volts
    b. 14 volts
    c. 12 volts
    d. 8 volts

7. If you wanted to measure how tight a bolt or a nut was, which one of the following tools would be the best choice for that?
    a. torque wrench
    b. screwdriver
    c. tight checker
    d. tape measure

8. What is a hand drill best used for?
    a. driving nails
    b. making holes in metal
    c. making holes in wood
    d. fastening tools

9. What might you use to tighten the image shown below?

    a. hammer
    b. screwdriver
    c. metal drill
    d. drill press

10. Which part of the engine opens up in order to release the exhaust that has been created by combustion inside the cylinder?
    a. piston ring
    b. exhaust pipe
    c. intake valve
    d. exhaust valve

11. What is one of the components that you might find inside of a car battery that helps to produce the electricity the vehicle uses?
    a. muriatic acid
    b. sulfuric acid
    c. hydrochloric acid
    d. heavy peroxide

12. Emissions are the method through which vehicles get rid of their exhaust into the atmosphere. This can be potentially damaging to the environment as a whole. Which of the following is meant to help control emissions in vehicles?
    a. catalytic converter
    b. pump
    c. flywheel
    d. windshield

13. When you buy motor oil for your engine, there is frequently a W in the type of viscosity the oil is rated for. What does that W stand for? Example: 5W-20.
    a. windy
    b. wind chill
    c. winter
    d. water resistance

14. What type of fastener would you commonly use to hold two pieces of wood together for a quick and dirty project?
    a. nails
    b. screws
    c. bolts
    d. glue

15. How is the gasoline that reaches the cylinders of the engine controlled?

    a. ignition

    b. fuel tank

    c. throttle

    d. brake system

16. The steering wheel uses the _____ to turn the wheels/

    a. engine

    b. tie rod

    c. transmission

    d. brake system

17. The image below represents an important part of vehicles. What part is it:

    a. engine

    b. undercarriage

    c. fuel system

    d. transmission

18. Which of the following systems applies friction to the wheels of a vehicle?
    a. brake system
    b. transmission
    c. drums and pads
    d. padding system

19. What is used to create the combustion inside of an engine?
    a. fuel tank
    b. gasoline and air
    c. gas pedal
    d. oil and air

20. Force applied to an object causing it to twist is called what:
    a. twist force
    b. friction
    c. turning power
    d. torque

21. What needs to be added to the radiator of an engine?
    a. water and coolant
    b. water
    c. water and ice
    d. radiator replacement fluid

22. What is shown below?

   a. staples
   b. hammers
   c. nails
   d. screws

23. Which of the following is used in the engine to prevent metal parts from rubbing against one another and causing damage?

   a. rubber
   b. oil
   c. coolant
   d. air

24. What is one of the possible uses for a wrench?

   a. loosen a nut
   b. tighten a screw
   c. break metal down into smaller parts
   d. fix a piece of wood

25. What helps you guide the way that the material goes through a table saw?

   a. fence
   b. gutter
   c. saw blocker
   d. both hands at the same time

MECHANICAL COMPREHENSION

1. What is the formula that is used to calculate work?
    a. W = F * s
    b. W = v * F
    c. W = P * s
    d. W = P * F

2. If an engine with a power output of around 2 horsepower is 95% efficient, what would the actual power output be, in horsepower?
    a. 190
    b. 95
    c. 1.90
    d. 0.19

3. A class 2 lever has the load placed between the fulcrum/pivot point and the effort being placed on it. Which of these might be an example of this?
    a. wheelbarrow
    b. gun
    c. wrench
    d. screwdriver

4. One of the following materials is a ceramic, which one is it?
    a. dirt
    b. gold
    c. pots
    d. brick

5. Force per unit of distance is a description of what?
    a. velocity
    b. force fields
    c. power
    d. work

6. Which one of the following might be a good example of a simple machine?
   a. ladder
   b. drill
   c. jackhammer
   d. iPod

7. A machine is operating with an input (for work) of 215-foot pounds. The output of the work for this machine is 204.25-foot pounds. What efficiency does this machine have, considering the information above?
   a. 90%
   b. 95%
   c. 100%
   d. 200%

8. If there are 20 lbs. on one side of a fulcrum (with equal lengths on both sides), which of the following combinations of weights would be enough to balance the loads on that fulcrum?
   a. 18 and 1
   b. 18 and 2
   c. 18 and 3
   d. 12 and 18

9. What kind of machine would a cam be considered?
   a. difficult
   b. simple
   c. conductor
   d. compound

10. How would you find an exerted force?
    a. find the force using the formula for work
    b. use the force field formula
    c. multiply applied force by the ratio of the areas to which it is being applied
    d. none of the above

11. What is a linkage?
    a. a way of converting rotating motion of a crank
    b. a type of fence
    c. a way to move chains
    d. a pulley system of complex design

12. Which of the following is a description of mechanical advantage?
    a. input force * output force
    b. output force * input force
    c. output force / input force
    d. input force / output force

13. If someone puts in 50 newtons of force and gets back 250 newtons of force, then what is the mechanical advantage?
    a. 5
    b. 10
    c. 15
    d. 20

14. What is the name of the force between objects that attracts them together?
    a. friction
    b. gravity
    c. force
    d. power

15. What might cause an object to accelerate?
    a. force
    b. gravity
    c. pulling on it
    d. all of the above

16. What amount of force would have to be applied to move a box 25 meters? 55,000 joules worth of work is utilized in the process of moving the box.
    a. 2500 newtons
    b. 4000 newtons
    c. 2200 newtons
    d. 5500 newtons

17. What is heat?
    a. a type of motion
    b. a type of pressure
    c. a type of energy
    d. the result of friction

18. If two liquids that have different densities are mixed together, what will happen?
    a. they will separate
    b. they will combine into one fluid
    c. they will react violently
    d. they will flow out of the container

19. What is the SI unit that is commonly used to measure mass?
    a. liter
    b. kilograms
    c. newtons
    d. all of the above

20. When would a spring likely be utilized?
    a. when making a large volleyball
    b. when creating a football
    c. when making a new baseball bat
    d. when building a pogo stick

21. When people are using a seesaw, the seesaw will work most efficiently if the two people have the same weight. Why?
    a. principle of equilibrium
    b. principle of force
    c. Newton's law
    d. the first law of motion

22. Shock absorption on vehicles is attributed to what?
    a. elasticity of springs
    b. brakes
    c. the engine block
    d. the weight of the vehicle

23. What type of device would you compare a crane to?
    a. car
    b. elevator
    c. pulley
    d. lever

24. If you were going to make something that was solid but would not float, what might you use?
    a. plastic
    b. glass
    c. metal
    d. wood

25. How do brakes slow vehicles down?
    a. force
    b. combustion
    c. acceleration
    d. friction

ASSEMBLING OBJECTS

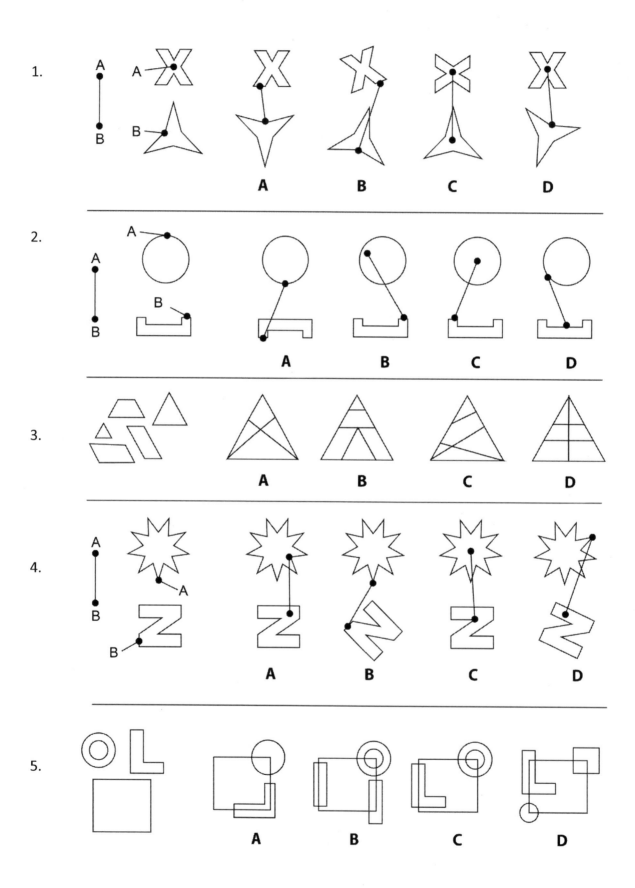

1.

A — B

A   B   C   D

2.

A — B

A   B   C   D

3.

A   B   C   D

4.

A — B

A   B   C   D

5.

A   B   C   D

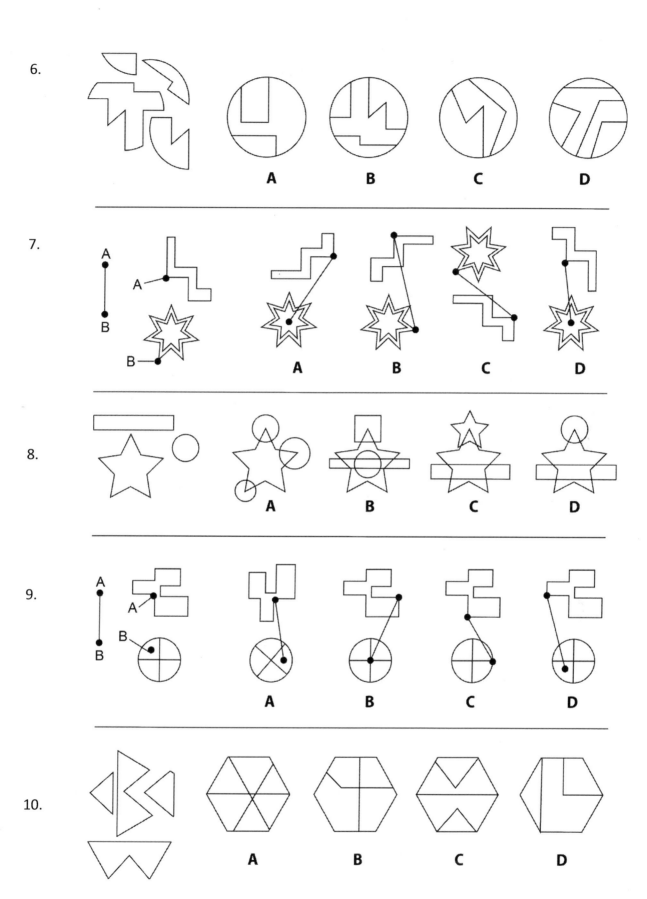

6.

7.

8.

9.

10.

63

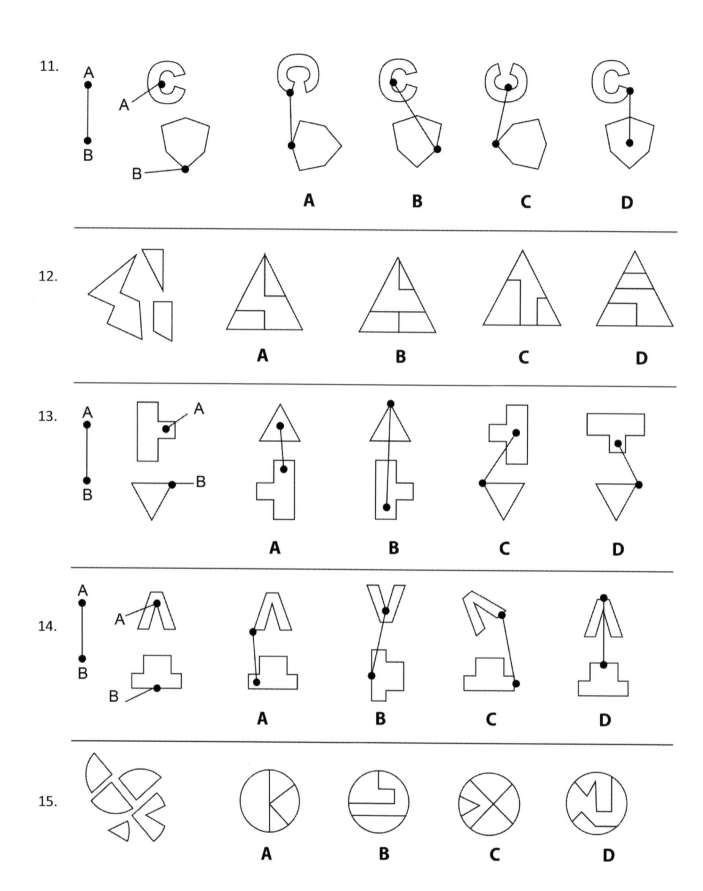

11.

A
B

A
B

A   B   C   D

12.

A   B   C   D

13.

A
B

A
B

A   B   C   D

14.

A
B

A
B

A   B   C   D

15.

A   B   C   D

16.

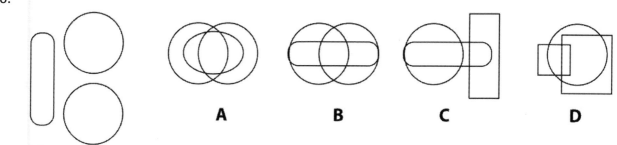

A

B

C

D

Practice Test #1 Answers

GENERAL SCIENCE

1. C.
2. A.
3. D.
4. B.
5. A.
6. B.
7. A.
8. C.
9. B.
10. C.
11. D.
12. B.
13. A.
14. B.
15. C.
16. A.
17. D.
18. C.
19. D.
20. D.
21. B.
22. A.
23. C.
24. B.
25. A.

ARITHMETIC REASONING

1. B.
2. C.
3. D.
4. D.
5. A.
6. D.
7. B.
8. B.
9. C.
10. A.
11. D.
12. D.
13. B.
14. C.
15. D.
16. D.
17. B.
18. A.
19. C.
20. C.
21. B.
22. D.
23. A.
24. A.
25. A.
26. D.
27. A.
28. A.
29. A.
30. C.

WORD KNOWLEDGE

1. D.
2. C.
3. A.
4. D.
5. A.
6. B.
7. C.
8. B.
9. C.
10. C.
11. A.
12. D.
13. B.
14. D.
15. C.
16. A.
17. B.
18. B.

19. A.
20. D.
21. C.
22. B.
23. A.
24. B.
25. C.
26. D.
27. A.
28. B.
29. D.
30. B.
31. C.
32. D.
33. C.
34. B.
35. B.

PARAGRAPH COMPREHENSION

1. C.
2. B.
3. D.
4. C.
5. A.
6. A.
7. B.
8. C.
9. D.
10. A.
11. B.
12. D.
13. A.
14. D.
15. D.

MATHEMATICS KNOWLEDGE

1. B.
2. B.
3. A.
4. B.
5. B.
6. B.
7. A.
8. D.
9. A.
10. D.
11. C.
12. D.
13. B.
14. C.
15. D.
16. A.
17. B
18. B.
19. B.
20. B.
21. C.
22. C.
23. B.
24. C.
25. C.

ELECTRONICS INFORMATION

1. D.
2. B.
3. A.
4. A.
5. C.
6. D.
7. A.
8. B.
9. C.
10. B.
11. D.
12. A.
13. A.
14. B.
15. C.
16. B.
17. D.
18. A.
19. A.
20. C.

AUTO & SHOP INFORMATION

1. A.
2. D.
3. D.
4. B.
5. B.
6. C.
7. A.
8. C.
9. B.
10. D.
11. B.
12. A.
13. C.
14. A.
15. C.
16. B.
17. D.
18. A.
19. B.
20. D.
21. A.
22. C.
23. B.
24. A.
25. A.

MECHANICAL COMPREHENSION

1. A.
2. C.
3. A.
4. D.
5. D.
6. A.
7. B.
8. B.
9. D.
10. C.
11. A.
12. C.
13. A.
14. B.
15. D.
16. C.
17. C.
18. A.
19. B.
20. D.
21. A.
22. A.
23. B.
24. C.
25. D.

ASSEMBLING OBJECTS

1. D.
2. A.
3. B.
4. B.
5. C.
6. B.
7. B.
8. D.
9. A.
10. C.
11. C.
12. A.
13. D.
14. B.
15. C.
16. B.

GENERAL SCIENCE

1. Which of the following is not in the Kingdom Plantae?
   a. Cactus
   b. Algae
   c. Oak Tree
   d. Sunflower

2. What is the primary difference between a cell membrane and a cell wall?
   a. A cell membrane is flexible, and a cell wall is rigid.
   b. A cell membrane is not found in plants, whereas a cell wall is.
   c. A cell membrane is not found in animals, whereas a cell wall is.
   d. A cell membrane is composed of protein, whereas a cell wall is composed of sugar.

3. Plants are autotrophs, meaning that they:
   a. Consume organic material produced by animals
   b. They produce their own food
   c. They are able to move by themselves
   d. They can automatically transform from a seed into a plant.

4. Which of the following is *not* true of a virus?
   a. Viruses have DNA
   b. Viruses do not have a nucleus
   c. Viruses cannot survive without water
   d. Viruses can be infectious

5. In the digestive system, the majority of nutrients are absorbed in the:
   a. Esophagus
   b. Stomach
   c. Small Intestine
   d. Large Intestine

6. How many pairs of human chromosomes exist?
    a. 17
    b. 13
    c. 23
    d. 29

7. Animals engaging in a symbiotic relationship will do which of the following?
    a. Help each other survive
    b. Take one another's food
    c. Attack one another
    d. Eat each other

8. What organ system contains your skin?
    a. The respiratory system
    b. The epithelial system
    c. The lymphatic system
    d. The circulatory system

9. If a gene is expressed, then that means that:
    a. It is influencing a phenotype trait
    b. It is being copied into another set of DNA
    c. It will be passed on from mother to son
    d. The gene will produce some hormones

10. Which of the following structures is found in eukaryotes but not in prokaryotes?
    a. A cell wall
    b. Mitochondria
    c. A nuclear membrane
    d. Vacuoles

11. Upon touching a chair cushion and then a metal plate, John notices that the metal plate feels much colder than the cushion, although the surrounding air temperature is the same. What is an explanation for this?
    a. The chair cushion has a higher heat capacity than the metal plate.
    b. The metal plate has a higher heat transfer rate than the chair cushion.
    c. The metal plate is able to absorb more heat from the air than the cushion.
    d. The chair cushion produces some internal heat.

12. If a pitcher throws a baseball into the air and notices that it takes 5 seconds to reach its peak, how long will the baseball need to fall back to the ground? Neglect air resistance.
    a. 2.5 seconds
    b. 9.8 seconds
    c. 5.0 seconds
    d. 10.0 seconds

13. Which of the following is correct regarding an aqueous substance?
    a. It is soluble in water
    b. It is very reactive
    c. It is soluble in hydrocarbon
    d. It is able to dissolve most other compounds

14. In order for work to be performed, a force has to be:
    a. Applied to an object
    b. Applied to a surface
    c. Applied to a moving object
    d. Applied over a distance to an object.

15. During which of the following geologic periods did the majority of life develop?
    a. Triassic
    b. Permian
    c. Cretaceous
    d. Cambrian

16. The nearest star to the sun is about 4.2 light-years away and is known as:
    a. Alpha Centauri
    b. Barnard's Star
    c. Sirius A
    d. Proxima Centauri

ARITHMETIC REASONING

1. Which of the following inequalities is true?
   a. 0.123 > 0.234
   b. -0.15 < -0.26
   c. -0.58 > 0.876
   d. -0.13 > -0.293

2. If you take 25% of 20, what would the resulting number be?
   a. 20
   b. 25
   c. 15
   d. 5

3. The average height of female students in a class is 64.5 inches, and the average height of male students in the class is 69 inches. If there are 1.5 times as many female students as male students, what is the average height for the entire class?
   a. 67.2 inches
   b. 66.75 inches
   c. 67.5 inches
   d. 66.3 inches

4. Meg rolled a 6-sided die 4 times, and her first 3 rolls were 1, 3, and 5. If the average of the 4 rolls is 2.5, what was the result of her fourth roll?
   a. 1
   b. 2
   c. 3
   d. 5

5. A parallelogram is divided into 2 triangles by drawing a straight line from one corner to an opposite corner. Which of the following is true of the 2 triangles?
   a. One triangle is an 180° rotation of the other.
   b. One triangle is a 90° rotation of the other.
   c. One triangle is an 180° reflection of the other.
   d. One triangle is a 90° translation of the other.

6. Jesse rides her bike 2 miles south and 8 miles east. She then takes the shortest possible route back home. What was the total distance she traveled?
   a. 17.75 miles
   b. 18.25 miles
   c. 8.25 miles
   d. 7.75 miles

7. Point A is *x* distance north of point B. Point C is east of point B and is twice as far from point B as point A is. What is the distance from point A to point C?
    a. $5x$
    b. $\sqrt{3}x$
    c. $2x$
    d. $\sqrt{5}x$

8. To get to school, Kaitlin walks 4 blocks north from her house, then turns right and walks 5 blocks east. How much shorter would her walk be if she could walk in a straight line from her house to her school?
    a. 6.4 blocks
    b. 3.2 blocks
    c. 6.0 blocks
    d. 2.6 blocks

9. A car rental company charges a daily fee of $48 plus 25% of the daily fee for every hour the car is late. If you rent a car for 2 days and bring it back 2 hours late, what will be the total charge?
    a. $120
    b. $108
    c. $72
    d. $144

10. There are 450 students in the 10th grade; of these, 46% are boys. If 21% of the girls have already turned 16, how many girls in the 10th grade are 16?
    a. 47
    b. 94
    c. 51
    d. 10

11. Solve $(3 + 5)^2 + 24 \div 16 - 5 \div 2$
    a. 0.25
    b. 30.25
    c. 33
    d. 63

12. A marinade recipe calls for 2 tablespoons of lemon juice for every $\frac{1}{4}$ cup of olive oil. How much lemon juice would be used with $\frac{2}{3}$ cup olive oil?
    a. $5\frac{1}{3}$ tablespoons
    b. $\frac{3}{4}$ tablespoons
    c. 4 tablespoons
    d. $2\frac{1}{3}$ tablespoons

13. Put the following integers and fractions in order from smallest to largest:
$0.125, \frac{6}{9}, \frac{1}{7}, 0.60$

    a. $\frac{1}{7}, 0.125, \frac{6}{9}, 0.60$

    b. $\frac{1}{7}, 0.125, 0.60, \frac{6}{9}$

    c. $0.125, \frac{1}{7}, 0.60, \frac{6}{9}$

    d. $\frac{1}{7}, 0.125, \frac{6}{9}, 0.60$

14. Megan cuts her birthday cake into 16 pieces. She and her 3 friends each eat a piece, and then Megan's dad eats $\frac{1}{3}$ of what is remaining. What fraction of the cake is left?

    a. $\frac{13}{24}$

    b. $\frac{1}{2}$

    c. $\frac{1}{4}$

    d. $\frac{3}{4}$

15. How many digits are in the sum $951.4 + 98.908 + 1.053$?

    a. 4

    b. 5

    c. 6

    d. 7

16. Simplify: 0.08×0.12

    a. 0.0096

    b. 0.096

    c. 0.96

    d. 9.6

WORD KNOWLEDGE

1. The soldiers engaged in <u>defensive</u> maneuvers to protect themselves from the enemy.
   a. Offensive
   b. Aggressive
   c. Protective
   d. Belligerent

2. Tenacious most nearly means:
   a. Surrendering
   b. Disloyal
   c. Persistent
   d. Thoughtful

3. Complacent most nearly means:
   a. Careless
   b. Careful
   c. Passionate
   d. Unconcerned

4. Fidelity most closely means:
   a. Falsity
   b. Treachery
   c. Separation
   d. Loyalty

5. The speech was <u>succinct</u>.
   a. Long
   b. Dull
   c. Exciting
   d. Short

6. Venerate most nearly means:
   a. Revere
   b. Admire
   c. Slander
   d. Desecrate

7. The <u>pivotal</u> moment in the battle changed the course of the war.
   a. Urgent
   b. Critical
   c. Minor
   d. First

8. Amicable most closely means:
   a. Unfriendly
   b. Angry
   c. Friendly
   d. Honest

9. He <u>feigned</u> interest when questioned.
   a. Expressed
   b. Pretended
   c. Celebrated
   d. Raised

10. She <u>reigned</u> for 27 years.
    a. Hid
    b. Worked
    c. Waited
    d. Ruled

11. Coup most nearly means:
    a. Takeover
    b. Henhouse
    c. Cover
    d. Failure

12. Abate most closely means:
    a. Increase
    b. Replace
    c. Decrease
    d. Worsen

13. Their efforts were in <u>vain</u>.
   a. Conceited
   b. Useless
   c. Effective
   d. Practical

14. The <u>yield</u> was better than expected.
   a. Revenue
   b. Surrender
   c. Outcome
   d. Product

15. Compel most closely means:
   a. Force
   b. Free
   c. Encourage
   d. Discourage

16. Advocate most nearly means:
   a. Adversary
   b. Enemy
   c. Friend
   d. Supporter

PARAGRAPH COMPREHENSION

1. Examples of colloquialisms include Facebook, y'all, gotta, and shoulda. What is the definition of a colloquialism?
    a. Words that are only used by Americans who live in the south.
    b. Words that only uneducated people say.
    c. Words that are used in an informal conversation, not a more formal discussion.
    d. Words that have recently been added to the dictionary as acceptable words to use in the American English Language.

2. Lieutenant Hiroo Onoda was a Japanese soldier who was sent to a small island in 1944 as an emissary. He refused to believe that Japan surrendered in WWII until his commanding officer finally traveled back to the island in 1974 and finally convinced him that the defeat was real. He then returned to Japan and received a hero's welcome.

    In this sentence what is the definition of emissary?
    a. Emissary refers to Hiroo Onoda being an ambassador for the Japanese army.
    b. In this sentence, emissary means a secret agent or spy.
    c. The word emissary means messenger in this sentence.
    d. Emissary, in the context of this sentence, means a delegate of the Japanese government meant to establish an embassy on the island.

3. Milton S. Hershey was the founder of North America's largest chocolate manufacturer, now known as, The Hershey Company. It is hard to believe that, with such a large, successful business, that Hershey's first attempts in the confectionary business were such failures. After finishing a confectionary apprenticeship, he opened his own candy shop in Philadelphia; 6 years later it went out of business. He then returned home after failing to manufacture candies in New York City and in 1903 construction of a chocolate plant began in his hometown which was later renamed Hershey, Pennsylvania.

    What is the main message of this passage?
    a. As an entrepreneur, if your first idea fails, do not give up, but move on to your next plan for success.
    b. One can only be successful in starting a flourishing business with the support of your hometown.
    c. It is more successful to manufacture chocolate than candy.
    d. If you start a worldwide profitable business in your hometown, they will rename the town in your honor.

4. *"Beware the leader who bands the drums of war in order to whip the citizenry into a patriotic fervor, for patriotism is indeed a double-edged sword."* This quote of Caesar's is completely anachronistic.

   What does anachronistic mean in this context?
   a. This word means stolen in this sentence. This is a quote from another ruler from the time of Caesar, but not Caesar himself.
   b. Anachronistic means a quote that is pieced together from parts of speeches made by an individual. It is, therefore, a quote without any real meaning.
   c. In this sentence, the word anachronistic means that this is a true and accurate quote; not a paraphrase.
   d. The word anachronistic is defined as a quote that is not historically accurate in its context. At the time of Caesar; there were no drums of war, for example.

5. *"A stitch in time saves nine."* This is a proverbial expression that has used for hundreds of years. What is this phrase referring to?
   a. This expression means that there is a "rip" of some sort in time and space and that only by repairing this rip will we save the world.
   b. When this phrase is used, the person means that by repairing a piece of clothing, you will save $9.00 on replacing the garment.
   c. This phrase refers to a broken relationship. If it is not repaired in time, it will take years (maybe even 9 years) to mend.
   d. The literal meaning of this expression means that if you stitch something up in time, you will save 9 stitches later. In other words, if you don't procrastinate, and repair something as soon as it is required, you won't have a bigger or worse job to fix at a later time.

6. In the Shakespearean play, *Julius Caesar*, a soothsayer calls out to Caesar with the following quote; *"Beware the Ides of March!"*

   What did this declaration of the soothsayer mean?
   a. The soothsayer was warning the ruler of his impending betrayal and death at the hands of some of his most trusted men.
   b. This phrase was actually warning the crowd, not Caesar that on ever Ides of March the ruler must choose one human sacrifice to offer up to the Roman gods to guarantee prosperity for the coming year.
   c. The Ides of March was a day of celebration in the Roman Empire to commemorate the deaths of the Christians in the Coliseum. The soothsayer was merely thanking Caesar for the day of celebration. The word "Beware" has been shown to be translated incorrectly into English.
   d. The soothsayer meant to warn Caesar not to upset or anger the god for whom the month of March was named; Mars, the god of war. To upset the god Mars, was to ensure plague, famine, or other ruin.

7. Tornados occur when air begins to rotate and comes into contact with both the earth and a cloud at the same time. Although the size and shape of tornados vary widely, one can usually see a funnel stretching from the sky down to land. Most tornados are accompanied with winds as fast as 110 miles per hour and extreme ones can have winds as fast as 300 miles per hour. The path of a tornado is hard to predict, but it is becoming possible to detect them just before or as they form with the continued collection of data through radar and "storm chasers". Storm chasing is a dangerous profession so why do people continue to put their lives in danger this way?
   a. Storm Chasers are an interesting breed of people who seek the thrill and adventure that comes along with this profession, much like extreme sports.
   b. News channels will pay large sums of money for good video of tornados, so, although it is a dangerous profession, the money is worth the risk.
   c. It is very important to discover as much as possible about how tornados work so that ultimately, scientists will detect them earlier and give people more advanced warning to get to safety. More advanced warning is the only way more lives will be saved.
   d. For statistics reasons, it is important to get first-hand data during a tornado. This way they can be compared to other natural disasters such as hurricanes and tsunamis.

8. "Secret Santa Sings Special Song for Sweetheart" is an example of alliteration. What does "alliteration" mean?
    a. Alliteration means that the sentence has more than one meaning.
    b. Alliteration means that people with a stutter would have difficulty saying this sentence.
    c. Alliteration means that most of the words in the sentence begin with the same letter.
    d. In this sentence "alliteration" means that a secret Santa *literally* sang a special song for his sweetheart; it means that this even actually happened.

9. The Schneider Family was not your average family. Three generations lived in one house; Mom and Dad, four of their children, and Mom's parents who were well into their "golden years." The term "golden years" is a nice way of meaning what?
    a. The term "golden years" refers to the best years of someone's life.
    b. This phrase means that the mom's parents were old or elderly people.
    c. "Golden years" is another way of saying, when they were rich.
    d. In this paragraph, the meaning of the term "golden years" means that the grandparents were spending their years taking care of everyone else in the family.

10. Jim had been on the road for 36 hours straight to meet an important client and hopefully finalize a huge new account for his advertising agency. After checking into his hotel, he intended just to drop off his suitcases and go down to the restaurant for a late supper. Once he entered the room, however, the cozy couch looked so friendly and welcoming to the weary traveler. Personification is a literary device that gives human characteristics to a non-human object.

    What phrase in this paragraph is an example of personification?
    a. An example from this paragraph that is personification is, "the cozy couch looked so friendly and welcoming...."
    b. "Jim had been on the road for 36 hours straight...." is an example of personification in this paragraph.
    c. The phrase, "...and hopefully, finalize a huge new account for his advertising agency." is an example of personification.
    d. An example of personification, in this paragraph, is, "...to just drop off his suitcase and go down to the restaurant...."

11. Of the phrases below, which one is an example of an oxymoron?
    a) Three of the employees were "let go" due to suspicion of stealing money from the cash drawer.
    b) The stormy night was perfect for this woman's current mood.
    c) It was raining "cats and dogs" when the school bell rang.
    d) The community center was collecting "useless treasures" for their upcoming garage sale.

MATH KNOWLEDGE

1. F(x)=6x-3, G(x)=3x+4

   What will be F(3)-G(2) equal to?
   - a. 4
   - b. 3
   - c. 5
   - d. 2

2. The mean of the marks obtained by the students in a class is 60 out of 100, and the standard deviation is 0. It means that
   - a. Half of the students have scored marks less than 60
   - b. Half of the students have scored marks greater than 60
   - c. No student has scored 100 marks
   - d. All the students have scored 60 marks each

3. 0.00092×10^{-3} is equal to which of the following?
   - a. 0.000093×10^{-4}
   - b. 0.000092×10^{-2}
   - c. 0.000000092
   - d. 0.92×10^{-8}

4. The remainder is 3 when we divide one number by another number. What can be these two numbers from the following?
   - a. 9, 5
   - b. 8, 5
   - c. 9, 6
   - d. both B & C

5. If A and B are odd integers. Which of the following expressions must give an odd integer?
   - a. A×B
   - b. A+B
   - c. A-B
   - d. Both options A & C

6. $\frac{4}{5} \div \text{.........} = 2$

   Which of the following will fill the blank?
   - a. $\frac{2}{5}$
   - b. $\frac{5}{2}$
   - c. $\frac{1}{5}$
   - d. Both A & C

7. Given is a set {2, 4, 6, 8........50}

How many numbers in the given set are completely divisible by 3?

    a. 6

    b. 8

    c. 7

    d. 9

8. What will be the area of the shaded region in the given figure?

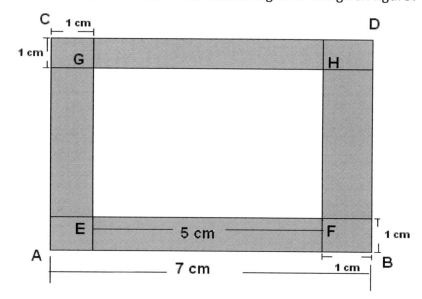

    a. 24 cm^2

    b. 26 cm^2

    c. 23 cm^2

    d. 28 cm^2

9. If 2x-y+6 = 2 then what will be the value of "6x"?

    a. 3y+12

    b. y-12

    c. y+12

    d. 3y-12

10. A point is located in coordinate system at (1, 2). What will be the location of this point if it is shifted 5 units downwards and 3 units in the right direction?

    a. (6, -1)

    b. (-4, 5)

    c. Remains same

    d. (4, -3)

11. $\dfrac{y+2}{3y^2+2y} + \dfrac{2y-1}{6y^3+4y^2} = $ ....

    a. $\dfrac{2y^2+6y-1}{6y^3+4y^2}$

    b. $\dfrac{2y^2+8y-1}{6y^3+4y^2}$

    c. $\dfrac{2y^2+6y-1}{3y^2+2y}$

    d. $\dfrac{2y^2+8y-1}{3y^2+2y}$

12. If each side of the square has been increased by 1 cm and the area has now become 36cm². What will be the length of one side of the square before?

    a. 4 cm

    b. 5 cm

    c. 6 cm

    d. 7 cm

13. $(9)^{-3} = $ ....

    a. $\dfrac{1}{9}$

    b. $-\dfrac{1}{(9)^3}$

    c. $\dfrac{1}{(9)^{-3}}$

    d. $\dfrac{1}{(9)^3}$

14. What is the degree of polynomial $5x^2y-5x^2y^2+5x^3y^2$?

    a. 12

    b. 4

    c. 8

    d. 5

15. Which one of the following numbers is not divisible by 3?

    a. 2352

    b. 3243

    c. 6143

    d. 5232

16. $(3-x)(3+x) = $ ....

    a. $9-x^2$

    b. x^2-9

    c. $9+x^2$

    d. x^2-6x+9

ELECTRONICS INFORMATION

1. Which one of the following is the correct relation between Power (P), Voltage (V) and Current (I)?
   a. P = V/I
   b. V = I/P
   c. P = VI
   d. P = I/V

2. What is the role of a rectifier?
   a. It converts AC to DC
   b. It steps up AC
   c. It converts DC to AC
   d. It steps up DC

3. Lagging power factor in an electrical circuit occurs due to the presence of which of the following?
   a. Capacitor
   b. Inductor
   c. Resistor
   d. Transistor

4. RL-circuit denotes which one of the following?
   a. Resistor-Capacitor Circuit
   b. Response-Lagging Circuit
   c. Reverse-Lagging Circuit
   d. Resistor-Inductor Circuit

5. The reverse recovery of a typical MOSFET is:
   a. Comparable to that of a BJT
   b. Faster than that of a BJT
   c. Slower than that of a BJT
   d. The reverse recovery of a typical MOSFET does not exist

6. A BJT, being used for amplification purpose in some applications, has:
   a. CB junction is reverse biased, and EB junction is forward biased
   b. CB junction is forward biased, and EB junction is also forward biased
   c. CB junction is reverse biased, and EB junction is also reverse biased
   d. CB junction is forward biased, and EB is reverse biased

7. Which of the following can be the applications of a transistor?
   a. Switching device
   b. Variable Resistor
   c. Amplifier
   d. All of the above

8. The DC current gain of the transistor (i.e. β) is represented as:
   a. I_B/I_C
   b. $I_B \times I_C$
   c. I_C/I_B
   d. $I_C - I_B$

9. The collector current in a transistor is regulated by which of the following?
   a. Base Current
   b. Emitter Current
   c. Input Resistance
   d. Output Resistance

10. Which one of the following statements is correct?
   a. The electrical conductivity of an intrinsic semiconductor is high as compared to that of an extrinsic semiconductor
   b. The electrical conductivity of an intrinsic semiconductor is low as compared to that of an extrinsic semiconductor
   c. The electrical conductivity of an intrinsic semiconductor is equal to that of an extrinsic semiconductor
   d. We cannot find a relationship between the electrical conductivity of intrinsic and extrinsic semiconductors.

11. Which one of the following describes the correct relationship between emitter current (I_E), Collector Current (I_C) and Base Current (I_B) of a transistor?
   a. $I_E = I_C - I_B$
   b. $I_E = I_B/I_C$
   c. $I_E = I_C + I_B$
   d. $I_E = I_C/I_B$

12. Two resistors of different values are connected in parallel to the supply voltage. Which of the following is the correct statement regarding this circuit?
   a. The resistance having a large value causes more power loss
   b. The resistance having a small value causes more power loss
   c. Both resistors cause same power loss
   d. We cannot calculate power loss with the given data

13. Which one of the following is the condition for an RLC circuit to be at resonance?
   a. $X_L = X_C$
   b. $X_L = R$
   c. $X_C = R$
   d. $X_L > X_C$

14. According to Ohm's Law, what will happen to the voltage if the resistance increases by 4 times and the current becomes half of its actual value?
   a. The voltage becomes half of its actual value
   b. The voltage remains same
   c. The voltage becomes twice of its actual value
   d. The voltage increases by 4 times of its actual value

15. Which one of the following statements is true regarding the characteristics of an ideal operational amplifier?
   a. An ideal operational amplifier has an infinite output impedance.
   b. An ideal operational amplifier has an infinite input impedance.
   c. An ideal operational amplifier has a finite bandwidth.
   d. All of the above

16. Which one of the following formulas depicts the output voltage of an inverting amplifier (where R_1 is the input resistance and R_2 is the output resistance)?
   a. $V_{out} = V_{in} \times (R_2/R_1)$
   b. $V_{out} = -V_{in} \times (R_1/R_2)$
   c. $V_{out} = V_{in} \times (R_1/R_2)$
   d. $V_{out} = -V_{in} \times (R_2/R_1)$

AUTO INFORMATION

1. A fuel-injected engine does not have:
   a. A fuel pump
   b. An intake valve
   c. A carburetor
   d. Either a or c

2. What device steps up the voltage delivered to the distributor?
   a. Contact Points
   b. Battery
   c. Spark Plug
   d. Ignition Coil

3. Which measurement can cause abnormal tire wear if not properly adjusted?
   a. Toe
   b. Camber
   c. Tire Pressure
   d. All of the above

4. Which of the following oils would be the thinnest at high temperatures?
   a. SAE 30
   b. 5W-20
   c. 5W-30
   d. 10W-40

5. Which of the following lists the stages of a four stroke engine cycle in the correct order?
   a. Compression, Intake, Exhaust, Power
   b. Suction, Compression, Power, Output
   c. Intake, Compression, Power, Exhaust
   d. Intake, Displacement, Ignition, Power

6. In which of the following engine configurations are the cylinders arranged in a single row?
   a. V
   b. Inline
   c. Flat
   d. Both a and c

7. What does antifreeze do?
    a. Raises the boiling point of water
    b. Lowers the boiling point of water
    c. Lowers the freezing point of water
    d. Both a and c

8. In which type of vehicle construction is the body not permanently mounted to the frame?
    a. Unibody
    b. Body-over-frame
    c. Monocoque
    d. All of the above

9. Which of these is not true of the power stroke?
    a. All valves are closed during the power stroke
    b. The power stroke occurs before the compression stroke
    c. Expanding gasses force the piston downward during the power stroke
    d. The spark plug ignites the air-fuel mixture to initiate the power stroke

10. What translates the linear motion of the piston to the rotation of the crankshaft in an engine?
    a. Torque Converter
    b. Connecting Rod
    c. Catalytic Converter
    d. Push Rod

11. What does the internal combustion engine burn?
    a. air
    b. Fuel
    c. Air-fuel mixture
    d. Alcohol

SHOP INFORMATION

1. What would be used to create external, or male, threads?
    a. Tap
    b. Die
    c. Thread gauge
    d. Calipers

2. Which of the following should not be used for tight bolts?
    a. Box end wrench
    b. Crescent wrench
    c. Breaker bar
    d. 6-point socket

3. Vernier calipers can be used to measure:
    a. Diameter
    b. Depth
    c. Thickness
    d. All of the above

4. Which of the following should be used to begin the removal of a spring pin?
    a. Drift punch
    b. Center punch
    c. Chisel
    d. None of the above

5. When arc welding, what is attached to the workpiece?
    a. Electrode
    b. Flux
    c. Ground clamp
    d. Filler rod

6. Which of the following wooden objects would be created on a lathe?
    a. Table top
    b. Frame
    c. Baseball bat
    d. Shelf

7. What is the purpose of a sanding block?
    a. Secure the workpiece while sanding
    b. Sanding within small crevices of a wooden object
    c. Smoothing the other surface of round objects
    d. Preventing an uneven finish when sanding

8. The mallet and sledge are examples of:
   a. Cutting tools
   b. Striking tools
   c. Splitting tools
   d. Flattening tools

9. What should be done when using a file?
   a. Apply pressure only on the forward stroke
   b. Secure a handle onto the pointed tang
   c. Hold the file with one hand on the handle and the other on the file tip
   d. All of the above

10. What tool would be best suited for holding a small electrical component in a small, confined space?
   a. Slip-joint pliers
   b. Vise-grips
   c. Needle-nose pliers
   d. Calipers

11. Which of following can be used to cut metal without the application of heat?
   a. Cold chisel
   b. Pin Punch
   c. Hot chisel
   d. Starting Punch

MECHANICAL COMPREHENSION

1. Which of the following is not a correct unit for the amount of work done:
   a. Joule
   b. Horsepower-hour
   c. Calorie
   d. Newton

2. Observe the figure:

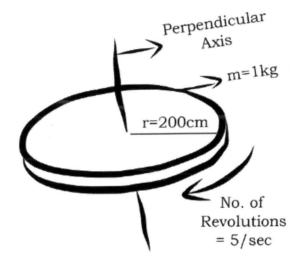

The kinetic energy of the disc is:
a. $80 \, \pi^2$ J
b. $100 \, \pi^2$ J
c. $125 \, \pi^2$ J
d. $144 \, \pi^2$ J

3. Consider the following figure of a rolling wheel on smooth horizontal surface:

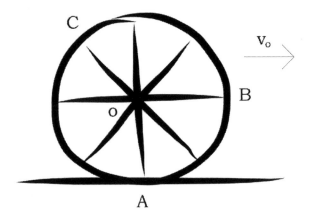

Then,

    i.   Speed at the point A is 0
    ii.   Speed at point B & C = v_o
    iii. Speed at point B > Speed at point O

a. All the statements are true
b. Only statement (i) & (ii) are true
c. Only statement (i) & (iii) are true
d. Only statement (ii) & (iii) are true

4. In the following figure, consider a block of mass m. What is the ratio of the force required, for a person to lift the block upwards with & without a pulley? (Hint: Assume F=T)
    a. 2
    b. 1/3
    c. 3
    d. ½

5. A block of mass 3kg lies on a horizontal surface with $\mu = 0.7$, select the force closest to what is required just to move the block:
    a. 15N
    b. 21N
    c. 18N
    d. 24N

6. P is a block of mass 5kg. At point Q, a block of mass 3kg was attached just to slide the block P.

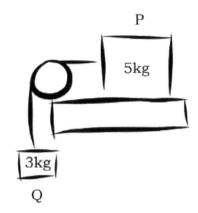

If no displacement occurs, the coefficient of friction between the block P and the horizontal surface is:

a. 0.5
b. 0.6
c. 0.7
d. 0.8

7. A ball is thrown into the air. After few seconds, it returns back to the earth. What can be its likely cause?
    a. Earth's gravitational field pulls it back
    b. It's speed did not match the escape velocity of earth
    c. Neither of these is correct
    d. Both (a) and (b) are correct

8. The factor which distinguishes between a scalar and a vector quantity is:
    a. Magnitude
    b. Direction
    c. Both (a) & (b)
    d. Neither (a) nor (b)

9. An athlete couldn't stop himself immediately after crossing the finish line. He was explained why this was happening by Newton's:
    a. 1st law of motion
    b. 2nd law of motion
    c. 3rd law of motion
    d. Law of Universal Gravitation

10. How is the weight of a person in an elevator affected if the elevator accelerates upwards, accelerates downwards and is at rest?
    a. Increases, Decreases, Remains Constant
    b. Decreases, Remains Constant, Increases
    c. Remains Constant, Increases, Decreases
    d. Decreases, Increases, Remains Constant

11. In the above example of a lift, which of Newton's law is demonstrated?
    a. 1st law of motion
    b. 2nd law of motion
    c. 3rd law of motion
    d. Law of Universal Gravitation

12. The threads of a screw work on the principle of another type of simple machine, which is:
    a. Lever
    b. Inclined plane
    c. Wedge
    d. None of the above

13. The shaft of the screw penetrates wood through the principle of yet another simple machine, which is:
    a. Inclined plane
    b. Lever
    c. Wedge
    d. None of the above

14. The following objects are an example of which order of the lever:
    Forceps, Scissors, Fishing Rod, Bottle Opener
    a. 3rd, 2nd, 3rd, 1st
    b. 2nd, 3rd, 1st, 3rd
    c. 3rd, 1st, 3rd, 2nd
    d. 1st, 3rd, 2nd, 3rd

15. A mechanic observes that he is able to lift the car by 2cm if he moves the lever down by 30cm. if he is applying a force of 20N to the lever, the force applied by the lever on the car is:
    a. 250N
    b. 300N
    c. 350N
    d. 400N

16. Angular momentum of a body doesn't change if:
    a. External torque is not applied
    b. External torque is applied in CW Direction
    c. External torque is applied in CCW Direction
    d. External torque has no effect on the angular momentum of the body

ASSEMBLING OBJECTS

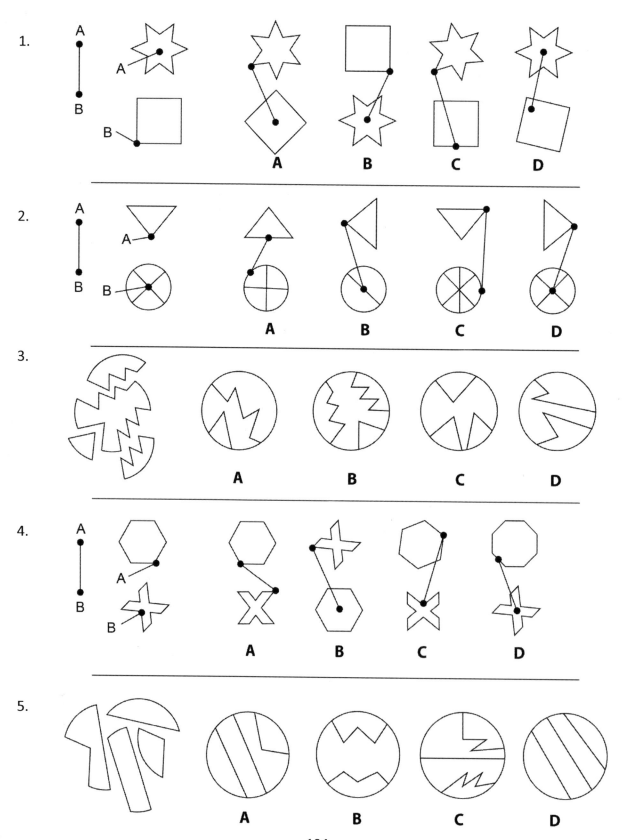

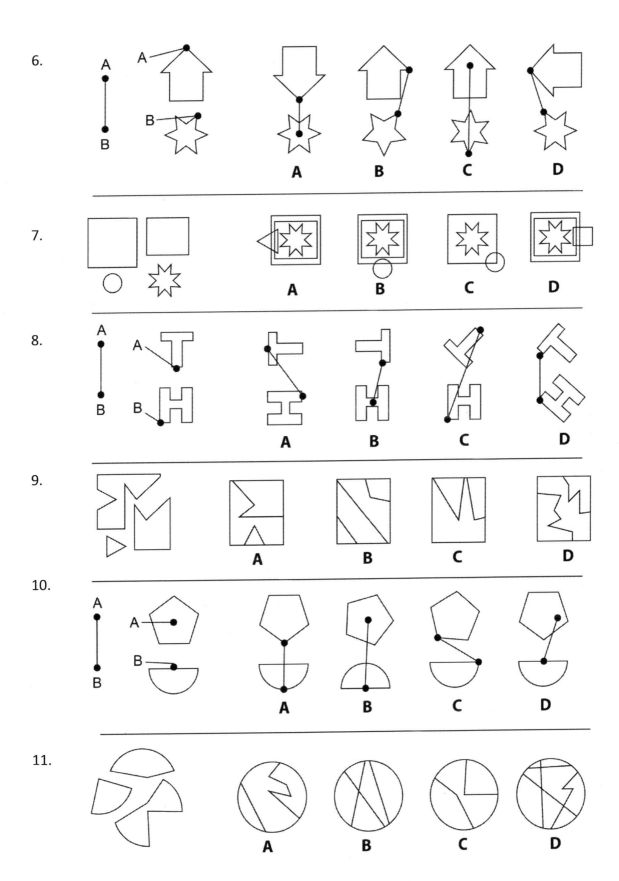

6.

7.

8.

9.

10.

11.

105

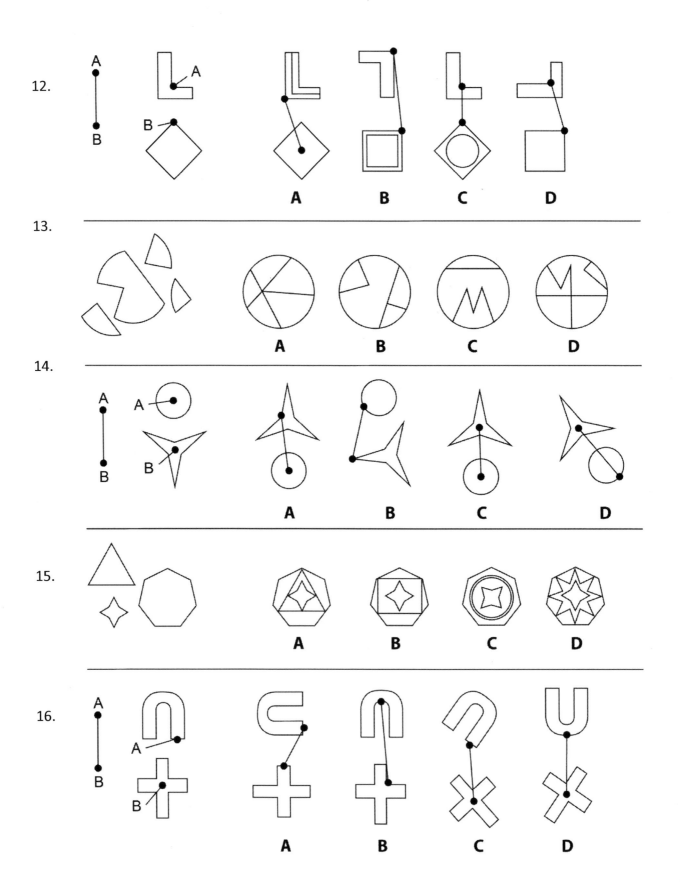

12.

A
B

A

B

A   **B**   **C**   **D**

13.

A   **B**   **C**   **D**

14.

A
B

A

B

A   **B**   **C**   **D**

15.

A   **B**   **C**   **D**

16.

A
B

A

B

A   **B**   **C**   **D**

106

Practice Test #2 Answers

GENERAL SCIENCE

1. B.
2. A.
3. B.
4. C.
5. C.
6. C.
7. A.
8. B.
9. A.
10. C.
11. B.
12. C.
13. A.
14. D.
15. D.
16. D.

ARITHMETIC REASONING

1. C.
2. B.
3. A.
4. D.
5. B.
6. A.
7. C.
8. C.
9. C.
10. B.
11. B.
12. B.
13. B.
14. B.
15. D.
16. A.

WORD KNOWLEDGE

1. C.
2. C.
3. D.
4. D.
5. D.
6. A.
7. B.
8. C.
9. B.
10. D.
11. A.
12. C.
13. B.
14. A.
15. A.
16. D.

PARAGRAPH COMPREHENSION

1. C.
2. B.
3. A.
4. D.
5. D.
6. A.
7. C.
8. C.
9. B.
10. A.
11. D.

MATH KNOWLEDGE

1. C.
2. D.
3. B.
4. D.
5. A.
6. A.
7. B.
8. A.
9. D.
10. D.
11. A.
12. B.
13. D.
14. D.
15. C.
16. A.

ELECTRONICS INFORMATION

1. C.
2. A
3. B.
4. D.
5. B.
6. A.
7. D.
8. C.
9. A.
10. B.
11. C.
12. B.
13. A.
14. C.
15. B.
16. D.

AUTO INFORMATION

1. C.
2. D.
3. D.
4. B.
5. C.
6. B.
7. D.
8. B.
9. B.
10. B.
11. C.

SHOP INFORMATION

1. B.
2. B.
3. D.
4. A.
5. C.
6. C.
7. D.
8. B.
9. D.
10. C.
11. A.

MECHANICAL COMPREHENSION

1. D.
2. B.
3. C.
4. D.
5. B.
6. B.
7. D.
8. B.
9. A.
10. A.
11. C.
12. B.
13. C.
14. C.
15. B.
16. A.

ASSEMBLING OBJECTS

1. B.
2. D.
3. B.
4. C.
5. A.
6. D.
7. B.
8. C.
9. A.
10. B.
11. C.
12. D.
13. B.
14. C.
15. A.
16. C.

GENERAL SCIENCE

1. A mutation in DNA can be caused by all of the following except:
    a. Ultraviolet radiation
    b. Chemical exposure
    c. DNA replication error
    d. Exonic duplication

2. People who suffer from Type I diabetes are lacking function in which organ?
    a. Liver
    b. Pancreas
    c. Stomach
    d. Heart

3. One of the primary differences between fungi and plants is that:
    a. Fungi can produce their own food and plants cannot.
    b. Plants have chlorophyll and fungi do not.
    c. Fungi are able to grow without water and plants cannot.
    d. Fungi and plants have no major differences.

4. Which of the following organisms is capable of asexual reproduction?
    a. Squash plant
    b. Amoeba
    c. Salmon
    d. Koala bear

5. In our atmosphere, nitrogen is the most common element, and makes up approximately what percentage?
    a. 25%
    b. 51%
    c. 65%
    d. 78%

6. In the human body, which of the following is responsible for clotting blood?
    a. Platelets
    b. White blood cells
    c. Red blood cells
    d. Osteoplasts

7. In plants, the female reproductive structures reside in the pistil, whereas the male reproductive structures are in the:
   a. Stamen
   b. Anther
   c. Sepals
   d. Petals

8. In the human body, communication occurring from cell to cell can happen through the use of:
   a. Neurotransmitters
   b. Pili
   c. Flagella
   d. ATP

9. In the following list, which would be considered to be at the top of the food chain?
   a. Snake
   b. Mouse
   c. Hawk
   d. Tomato plant

10. Tundra, rainforest, and prairie are all examples of ecological classifications known as:
    a. Ecomes
    b. Partitions
    c. Biomes
    d. Communities

11. According to electron theory, what is the maximum number of bonds a carbon atom can have?
    a. 2
    b. 3
    c. 4
    d. 5

12. If a rowboat weighs 50 kilograms, how much water needs to be displaced in order for the boat to float?
    a. 25 liters
    b. 50 liters
    c. 100 liters
    d. 500 liters

13. Given the reaction: $CaSO_4$ (aq) + $CuCl_2$ (aq) →, which of the following is a possible product?
    a. CaCl
    b. CaCu
    c. $CuSO_3$
    d. $CaCl_2$

14. A ball with a mass of 0.5 kg is moving at 10 m/s. How much kinetic energy does it have?
    a. 15 Joules
    b. 25 Joules
    c. 50 Joules
    d. 55.5 Joules

15. A volcano that is low and flat to the ground, and does not typically have large, violent eruptions can be classified as what?
    a. A plane volcano
    b. A cinder cone
    c. A shield volcano
    d. A screen volcano

16. Which of these types of rocks is created near or on the earth's surface?
    a. Igneous rock
    b. Sedimentary rock
    c. Crustaceous rock
    d. Metamorphic rock

ARITHMETIC REASONING

1. A car dealership is offering huge deals for the weekend. The commercials claim that this year's models are 20% off the list price, and the dealership will pay the first 3 monthly payments. If a car is listed for $26,580, and the monthly payments are set at $250, what are the total potential savings?
    a. $20,514
    b. $5,566
    c. $6,066
    d. $1,282

2. Joe baked brownies in a 9 inch × 11 inch × 2 inch tray. He then cut the brownies into 12 large pieces. Joe ate 2 pieces, his roommate ate 3 pieces, and the dog, unfortunately, ate half of what was remaining. How much of the brownies did the dog eat?
    a. 99 in^3
    b. 57.75 in^3
    c. 82.5 in^3
    d. 115.5 in^3

3. The county is instituting a new license plate system. The new plates will have 6 digits: the first digit will be 1, 2, or 3, and the next 5 digits can be any number from 0 – 9. How many possible unique combinations does this new system offer?
    a. 3×10^5
    b. 3×10^6
    c. 10^6
    d. 53

4. What percent of 14 is 35?
    a. 4.9%
    b. 2.5%
    c. 40%
    d. 250%

5. The high temperature on Wednesday is 4 degrees warmer than the high temperature on Tuesday, which was 5 degrees cooler than the high temperature on Monday. If the high temperature on Thursday is predicted to be 3 degrees cooler than the high on Wednesday, what is the difference in temperature between Monday and Thursday?
    a. 3 degrees
    b. 4 degrees
    c. 6 degrees
    d. 12 degrees

6. A dry cleaner charges $3 per shirt, $6 per pair of pants, and an extra $5 per item for mending. Annie drops off 5 shirts and 4 pairs of pants, 2 of which needed mending. Assuming the cleaner charges an 8% sales tax, what will be Annie's total bill?
   a. $52.92
   b. $49.00
   c. $45.08
   d. $88.20

7. A car dealership has sedans, SUVs, and minivans in a ratio of 6:3:1, respectively. In total, there are 200 of these vehicles on the lot. What proportion of those vehicles are sedans?
   a. 120
   b. $\dfrac{3}{100}$
   c. $\dfrac{3}{5}$
   d. $\dfrac{3}{10}$

8. A summer camp requires a ratio of 1 camp counselor to every 6 campers. Each camp counselor makes $480 per week. If the camp director wants to register an additional 30 campers for 2 weeks this summer, how much more will she have to budget to pay counselors?
   a. $2,400
   b. $4,800
   c. $5,760
   d. $2,880

9. Simplify: $\left(x^{1/2}\right)^{-3}$
   a. $x^{-1/2}$
   b. $x^{-5/2}$
   c. $\dfrac{1}{\sqrt{x^3}}$
   d. $\sqrt{x^3}$

10. A sporting goods store is offering an additional 30% off all clearance items. Angie purchases a pair of running shoes on clearance for $65.00. If the shoes originally cost $85.00, what was her total discount?
    a. 53.5%
    b. 46.5%
    c. 22.9%
    d. 39.2%

11. In July, gas prices increased by 15%. In August, they decreased by 10%. What is the total percent change since June?
    a. 5% increase
    b. 3.5% decrease
    c. 3.5% increase
    d. 1.5% increase

12. A bag contains twice as many red marbles as blue marbles, and the number of blue marbles is 88% of the number of green marbles. If g represents the number of green marbles, which of the following expressions represents the total number of marbles in the bag?
    a. $3.88g$
    b. $3.64g$
    c. $2.64g$
    d. $2.32g$

13. If 5 subtracted from 3 times x is greater than x subtracted from 15, which of the following is true of x?
    a. $x < -5$
    b. $x > 5$
    c. $x > 10$
    d. $x > -10$

14. Find the 10th term in the following sequence: $20, 8, -4, -16, \dots$
    a. -100
    b. -88
    c. -72
    d. -136

15. For which of the following functions does $f(x) = |f(x)|$ for every value of x?
    a. $f(x) = 3 - x$
    b. $f(x) = 2x + x^2$
    c. $f(x) = x^3 + 1$
    d. $f(x) = x^2 + (2 - x)^2$

16. A radio station plays songs that last an average of 3.5 minutes and has commercial breaks that last 2 minutes. If the station is required to play 1 commercial break for every 4 songs, how many songs can the station play in an hour?
    a. 15
    b. 11
    c. 16
    d. 17

17. They investigated the <u>alleged</u> human rights violations.
    a. Proven
    b. False
    c. Unproven
    d. Horrific

18. Cede most nearly means:
    a. Consign
    b. Surrender
    c. Keep
    d. Abandon

19. Afflict most closely means:
    a. Attack
    b. Perturb
    c. Assist
    d. Agonize

20. Conspicuous most nearly means:
    a. Bold
    b. Unremarkable
    c. Quiet
    d. Dull

21. <u>Insurgents</u> were responsible for a number of attacks, including suicide bombings.
    a. Anarchists
    b. Communists
    c. Rebels
    d. Patriots

22. Austere most nearly means:
    a. Welcoming
    b. Ornate
    c. Simple
    d. Fanciful

23. Admonish most closely means:
    a. Denounce
    b. Dislike
    c. Reprimand
    d. Praise

24. Deference most nearly means:
    a. Defiance
    b. Submissiveness
    c. Hostility
    d. Sociability

25. The site had been <u>neglected</u> for years.
    a. Ignored
    b. Maintained
    c. Crumbling
    d. Growing

26. Insinuate most closely means:
    a. Infiltrate
    b. Introduce
    c. Proclaim
    d. Abbreviate

27. Explicate most nearly means:
    a. Obscure
    b. Decipher
    c. Clarify
    d. Confuse

28. Decorum most nearly means:
    a. Propriety
    b. Decoration
    c. Drunkenness
    d. Indecency

29. He was <u>chagrined</u> when he tripped and fell in the hallway.
    a. Injured
    b. Embarrassed
    c. Unharmed
    d. Angry

30. Audacious most nearly means:
    a. Frightening
    b. Engaging
    c. Daring
    d. Boring

31. The <u>intrepid</u> volunteers worked in the refugee camps.
    a. Uncaring
    b. Caring
    c. Compassionate
    d. Fearless

32. Surreptitious most nearly means:
    a. Hidden
    b. Clandestine
    c. Public
    d. Illegal

PARAGRAPH COMPREHENSION

1. Every year the Academy Awards, or better known as The Oscars, brings together the best of the best in Hollywood. Each year since the original awards ceremony in 1929 great achievements in all areas of the film industry are recognized. Many married female actors, however, shy away from the honor of winning the *Academy Award of Merit* for either Best Actress or Best Supporting Actress. Ever since 1935, the "Oscar Curse" has proven more often than not to be alive and well.

   What is the "Oscar Curse" that these famous ladies of Hollywood fear?
   a. They fear that after winning they will meet an untimely end.
   b. That soon after winning this prestigious award, the lady's husband will leave them.
   c. The fear is that their next movie will be a box-office disaster.
   d. They fear that once they win one, they will never again win in the same category.

2. According to CNN.com, Google recently announced that it is developing smart contact lenses that will measure a diabetic's glucose level by testing the person's tears. If victorious, Google will eliminate a very laborious daily routine in every diabetic's life; drawing blood from their body (usually from the side of a finger) to test their glucose levels.

   In this paragraph, what does the word laborious mean?
   a. Consuming too much time
   b. Needing much unwelcome, often tedious, effort
   c. Needing to be done in a medical laboratory
   d. An excruciatingly painful procedure

3. Ikea stores have a unique section in their parking lots. They have a "family friendly" parking area. This area is located very close to the front entrance to the store. These spots have pink strollers painted on each parking spot. What is implied by the term "family friendly"?
    a. It is implying that only those customers who come to shop at the store with young children or pregnant women can park in this area.
    b. That if you have an Ikea Family Membership you are welcomed to park in this area.
    c. Any family, of any age, are welcome to park in this special area.
    d. That if there are only a few spots left in this area of the parking lot, it would be nice to leave it for a vehicle with a family but not it isn't necessary; anyone can park there.

4. Everyone dreams of winning the lottery; one million, 25 million, even 55 million dollars. It is very easy to get caught up in the dreams associated with winning the jackpot. The realists of the world, however, are quick to remind us that we have a better chance of being hit by a car than winning big with the lottery.

   What does the comparison of winning the lottery to being hit by a car imply?
    a. That if you don't have the good luck to win the lottery watch out because you only have bad luck and are likely to be hit by a car.
    b. It implies that it is not lucky to either win the lottery or be hit by a car.
    c. The comparison means that more people will get hit by a car than win big with the lottery.
    d. The implication is that if you are going to buy a lottery ticket, don't walk.

5. The United States Military Academy at West Point (USMA) is better known as The Point. Dating back to 1802, this coeducational federal service academy has trained some of the most revered and honored military leaders in American history. West Point has a Cadet Honor Code that is almost as old as the academy itself; "A Cadet will not lie, cheat, steal, or tolerate those who do."

    What is the foundation of the Honor Code of West Point?
    a. The foundation of the Honor Code comes from a time when the United States where divided by the conflicts leading up to the American Civil War, but were training soldiers from both sides of the Mason-Dixie Line. This Code was required to prevent men from fighting amongst themselves.
    b. This code came from the *Southern Gentleman's Guide to Behavior* and introduced to men from the northern states during the early years of the academy.
    c. The Honor Code of West Point was adopted from the *British Military's Training Manual* that was created years before West Point even existed.
    d. West Point's Code of Honor dates back to the beginning of the academy when a gentle man's word was considered his bond. To break one's word was the worst possible thing a gentleman could ever do. His word was his honor, and without honor a man was nothing.

6. Davy Crockett is one of America's best-known folk heroes. Known for his political contributions to the State of Tennessee and the U.S. Congress, he also became famous during his own time for "larger than life" exploits that were retold through plays and in almanacs. Even following his death, Davy Crockett became growingly famous for exploits of legendary magnitude.

    In this paragraph, what is the meaning of the word "almanacs"?
    a. An almanac is a book of information including a calendar, weather based predictions, anniversaries, and important events that is published yearly.
    b. An Almanac is another name for a book of locally developed plays that is published every couple years or so.
    c. An Almanac is a series of comics based on popular folklore that is published every five years.
    d. An almanac is a name given to stories that are handed down from one generation to another orally, not by written word.

7. Rosa Parks was a civil rights activist who refused to give up her seat in the colored section on a city bus for a white person when the white section of the bus was full and was subsequently arrested. *My Story*, which is her autobiography, she is quoted as saying, "People always say that I didn't give up my seat because I was [physically] tired [or] old....No, the only tired I was, was tired of giving in." What implied by this quote?
   a. That she was old and tired of walking home after work each day and finally gave in and paid to take the bus home.
   b. This quote implies that Rosa Parks was not tired physically, or too old to stand on a bus, she was just tired of having to give in to the demands of white people; she was tired of segregation based on race.
   c. This quote means that people thought Rosa Parks was just too lazy to give up her seat on the bus.
   d. Rosa Parks was just stubborn that day on the bus, and her actions had nothing to do with the civil rights movement.

8. One island from the shores of San Francisco Bay is often referred to as "The Rock"; Alcatraz Island. The island has been home to one kind of prison or another since 1861 up until 1963. During its time as a federal prison, it is stated that no prisoner successfully escaped from Alcatraz although there were 14 attempts in that time.

   Why were there never any successful escapes from the prison on Alcatraz Island?
   a. No one ever successfully escaped the prison because there were too many guards on duty. No man was ever left alone when outside of his cell.
   b. Alcatraz was inescapable because even if they penetrated the high-security around the prison, there was no way off the island since no boats were ever docked at the wharf.
   c. The entire premise of Alcatraz was that the men sent here were not to be rehabilitated back into society. Each and every aspect and component of the prison, the training of the guards, and the security around the rest of the island was created with the idea of keeping them on the island forever.
   d. The majority of men in the time the prison was active did not know how to swim, so those who attempted drowned in the water if they were not caught first.

9. When one wants to train a house-dog to ring a bell instead of barking to let its owner know it wants to go outside, there are only a few simple steps. First, when the dog is at the door, and barks take its paw and knock it against the bell that is hanging from the doorknob and only then open the door and let the dog outside. Repeat this every single time the dog barks to go outside. Eventually, depending on the stubbornness of the animal, the dog will cease barking at all and go to the bell and ring it each time it wants to go outside.

   What is the type of training called?
      a. This type of training is called Negative Behavior Elimination Training.
      b. This training is referred to as either Classical Conditioning or Pavlovian Conditioning.
      c. This training called Positive Reinforcement Training.
      d. This type of training is called Basic Cognitive Retraining.

10. When we think of "rights" we think in terms of Human Rights. This refers to ideas that apply to everyone, everywhere in the world. These expectations are egalitarian and are part of a declaration called the *Universal Declaration of Human Rights* that adopted by the U.N. General Assembly in 1948 after the end of WWII.

    In this paragraph, what does the word "egalitarian" mean?
      a. This word means that the rights contained in the *Universal Declaration of Human Rights* are to all be taken literally.
      b. Egalitarian means that ultimately these rights will also be applied to immediately to anyone and everyone who requests to be treated fairly.
      c. This word means that examples of basic human rights are included in the declaration adopted by the U.N.
      d. The word egalitarian means that Human Rights are the same for everyone, regardless of their race, nationality, or any other factors.

11. Each branch of the United States Armed Forces has special mottos that the soldiers live and are expected to die by. These special expressions are points of extreme pride for each member of the military. What is the motto of the United States National Guard?
    a. "This We'll Defend"
    b. "Always Ready, Always There"
    c. "That Others May Live"
    d. "Not Self, but Country"

MATH KNOWLEDGE

1. Which of these are parallel lines?
    a. x=2, y=3
    b. y=-1, x=4
    c. x=1, x=6
    d. x=9, y=100

2. Which of these are complementary angles?
    a. 63° and 29°
    b. 56° and 38°
    c. 33° and 57°
    d. 46° and 49°

3. The triangle whose one angle is greater than 90 degrees is called ....
    a. Equilateral Triangle
    b. Isosceles Triangle
    c. Scalene Triangle
    d. Obtuse Triangle

4. a×(b+c) = ...
    a. ab+bc
    b. cb+ac
    c. ab+ac
    d. abc

5. Which of the following options is true for Equilateral Triangle?
    a. Three Congruent Angles
    b. Three Congruent Sides
    c. Two Congruent Angles
    d. Two Congruent Sides

6. If $\frac{20-x}{4} = 3y$. What will be x in terms on y?
    a. 20-12y
    b. 20+12y
    c. 12-20y
    d. 12+20y

7. If 38 is divided by m then the remainder is 2 and the quotient is 12. What will be the value of "m" then?

     a. 2
     b. 3
     c. 5
     d. 4

8. If y = 7x, x = 3z. What will be the value of y if z = 2?

     a. 40
     b. 44
     c. 48
     d. 42

9. $4\frac{4}{6} + 2\frac{1}{3} - 1\frac{3}{4} \times 3\frac{2}{5} = $ ....

     a. $\frac{22}{20}$
     b. $\frac{24}{20}$
     c. $\frac{21}{20}$
     d. $\frac{25}{20}$

10. Which one of the following options shows the correct answer of y with respect to its equation?

     a. If 2(y-1)+6=0, then y= 2
     b. If 3(y-3)=3, then y=4
     c. If 2(y+2)=6, then y=-1
     d. If 6y-18 = 6, then y=5

11. A = x^2+3x-4, B = $2x^2$-2x+3. What will be the value of "B-A"?

     a. x^2-5x+7
     b. $3x^2$-x-1
     c. x^2-3x+7
     d. x^2-5x-7

12. Pythagorean Theorem is applicable to which one of the following triangles?

     a. Equilateral Triangle
     b. Acute Triangle
     c. Obtuse Triangle
     d. Right-Angled Triangle

13. x=3 is the solution of which one of the following equations?
   a. 6(x+3)-12 = 0
   b. 8(x-2)-4 = 0
   c. 7(x-6)+21 = 0
   d. 3(x+4)-9 = 0

14. There are two parallel lines x and y. One line s is passing through both these parallel lines such that <smk = 60°. What will be the value of angle k?

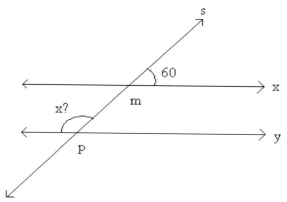

   a. 120°
   b. 60°
   c. 80°
   d. 150°

15. What will be the product of $3p^3-2p^2+p$ and $-2p$ will give?
   a. $-6p^4+4p^3-2p^2$
   b. $6p^4-4p^3+2p^2$
   c. $-6p^3+4p^2-2p$
   d. $6p^4+4p^3-2p^2$

16. We have two numbers x and y such that x+y=15, x-y=3. What will be the numbers?
   a. x=8, y=5
   b. x=10, y=7
   c. x=8, y=7
   d. x=9, y=6

ELECTRONICS INFORMATION

1. Which one of the following circuits is a high-pass filter?
   a. RC differentiator
   b. RL integrator
   c. RC integrator
   d. All of the above

2. The capacitor which shorts an Alternating Signal (AC) to ground is called:
   a. Motor Capacitor
   b. Bypass Capacitor
   c. Variable Capacitor
   d. None of these

3. FET stands for which of the following?
   a. Ferroelectric Transistor
   b. Ferromagnetic-effect Transistor
   c. Field-effect Transistor
   d. Ferrocene-electric Transistor

4. What is the relationship between voltage and current in case of a pure inductive circuit?
   a. Voltage is lagging Current by 90°
   b. Voltage is leading Current by 90°
   c. Current is leading Voltage by 90°
   d. Voltage is in phase with Current i.e. there is 0° angle between Current and Voltage

5. How many p-n junctions are there in a thyristor?
   a. 1
   b. 2
   c. 3
   d. 4

6. The terminals of a thyristor are:
   a. Emitter, Gate, Collector
   b. Anode, Gate, Cathode
   c. Emitter, Base, Collector
   d. Anode, Base, Cathode

7. Which one of the following options is not a region of operation of a BJT?
   a. Forward-Active Mode
   b. Saturation Mode
   c. Reverse-Blocking Mode
   d. Both options B and C

8. Thyristor is also known as which of the following?
   a. Silicon-Controlled Rectifier
   b. Sodium-Controlled Rectifier
   c. Sulfur-Controlled Rectifier
   d. Silicon-Controlled Rectifier

9. In which of the following regions of operation, the transistor acts as a switching device?
   a. Forward-Active Mode
   b. Saturation Mode
   c. Cut-off Mode
   d. Both options B and C

10. Which of the following statements is correct regarding BJT?
    a. The emitter is heavily doped as compared to the collector.
    b. BJT has four terminals
    c. While acting in forward-active mode, Collector-Base (C-B) junction is forward biased.
    d. Cut-off mode is mostly used for signal amplification.

11. Which one of the following statements is correct?
    a. MOSFET is a current-controlled device.
    b. BJT is a voltage-controlled device.
    c. Switching speed of a MOSFET is more than that of a BJT.
    d. Both options B and C

12. UPS stands for which of the following?
    a. Unidirectional Power Supply
    b. Uninterruptible Power Supply
    c. Unlimited Power Supply
    d. Unblocked Power Supply

13. The minority charge carriers in an n-type material are:
    a. Electrons
    b. Holes
    c. Neutrons
    d. Ions

14. How many electrons are present in the valence shell of a semi-conductor?
    a. 2
    b. 3
    c. 4
    d. 5

15. Which of the following statements is not correct regarding Zener Diode?
   a. Zener diode can be used as a voltage regulator.
   b. Zener diode can be used in the generation of reference voltage.
   c. Zener diode allows the current to flow in forward direction only.
   d. Zener diode can be used as an amplifier.

16. Two resistors of same value are connected in parallel to each other, the value of equivalent resistance will be:
   a. Less than the value of one resistor
   b. Greater than the value of one resistor
   c. The same as the value of one resistor
   d. Equal to the sum of both resistors

AUTO INFORMATION

1. The pitman arm is a component of which automotive system?
   a. Suspension System
   b. Exhaust System
   c. Steering System
   d. Brake System

2. What controls the spark timing in some cars?
   a. Distributor
   b. Camshaft
   c. Crankshaft
   d. Timing Chain

3. If spark timing is advanced at high rpm, the spark takes place _____.
   a. Earlier in the combustion cycle
   b. Later in the combustion cycle
   c. At the same time
   d. At a different location in the combustion chamber

4. What opens and closes the exhaust and intake valves?
   a. Connecting Rods
   b. Crankshaft
   c. Camshaft
   d. Flywheel

5. What is the normal mixture of water and anti-freeze in an engine's coolant?
   a. 30/70
   b. 50/50
   c. 70/30
   d. None of the above

6. Diesel engines have compression ratios between 14:1 and 23:1. Relative to gasoline engines, this is:
   a. Lower
   b. Higher
   c. Equal
   d. None of the above

7. What splits power between the front and rear axles on a four-wheel drive vehicle?
   a. Transmission
   b. Torque converter
   c. Transfer Case
   d. Differential

8. How many degrees does the camshaft turn for a complete revolution of the crankshaft in a four-stroke engine?
   a. 90
   b. 180
   c. 360
   d. 720

9. What helps recharge the battery and run electrical components while the engine is running?
   a. Distributor
   b. Alternator
   c. Ignition System
   d. Starter

10. What system controls the ride quality of a vehicle?
    a. Suspension System
    b. Steering System
    c. Safety System
    d. Fuel Delivery System

11. Which of the following oils would be the most viscous when starting in low temperature?
    a. SAE 10
    b. SAE 30
    c. 5W-20
    d. 10W-40

SHOP INFORMATION

1. What is the length of a 10 – 32 X 1 bolt?
   a. 10 mm
   b. 32 mm
   c. 1"
   d. 10"

2. What should be used to strike a chisel or punch?
   a. Rubber mallet
   b. Ball peen hammer
   c. Clawhammer
   d. All of the above

3. What type of hammer is used for assembling the frame of a house?
   a. Finishing hammer
   b. Sledgehammer
   c. Deadblow hammer
   d. Clawhammer

4. Which of the following is used for measuring a length?
   a. Tape rule
   b. Calipers
   c. Steel rule
   d. All of the above

5. What is the diameter of a 1/2 – 20 X 2 bolt?
   a. 1/2"
   b. 20 mm
   c. 2"
   d. 2 mm

6. Which of the following can be used for shaping wood?
   a. Chisel
   b. Plane
   c. Rasp
   d. All of the above

7. The value given by a pressure gauge is known as _____ pressure.
   a. Absolute
   b. Negative
   c. Gage
   d. Nominal

8. Which socket can be used with a 1/2" drive impact wrench?
   a. 1/4" flat black socket
   b. 1/2" blue titanium socket
   c. 3/4" chrome-plated socket
   d. 3/4" flat black socket

9. Which sandpaper would leave the smoothest finish?
   a. 20 grit
   b. 100 grit
   c. 140 grit
   d. 200 grit

10. What joining process would be used to bond two small electrical wires together?
    a. Brazing
    b. Oxyacetylene welding
    c. Soldering
    d. Arc welding

11. Which of these would give the most accurate measurement of a small part?
    a. Steel rule
    b. Calipers
    c. Micrometer
    d. Tape measure

MECHANICAL COMPREHENSION

1. Two moving bodies A & B possess the same amount of kinetic energy (see figure).

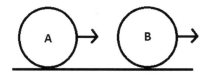

   If both the bodies are of unit mass then,
   a. Velocity of body A > Velocity of body B
   b. Velocity of body A = Velocity of body B
   c. Velocity of body A < Velocity of body B
   d. Cannot be determined, insufficient data

2. A flywheel, initially at rest, attains an angular velocity of 600rad/s in 15sec. Assuming constant angular acceleration, the angular displacement and angular acceleration of the flywheel in this time is:
   a. 4500rad, 40rad/s^2
   b. 5400rad, 40rad/s^2
   c. 4000rad, 45rad/s^2
   d. 4000rad, 54rad/s^2

3. The wedge angle of a particular wedge is increased. The Mechanical Advantage of the wedge:
   a. Increased
   b. Decreased
   c. Remained constant
   d. Any of the possibilities is likely as M.A. is not affected by the wedge angle

4. Calculate the Mechanical Advantage of the following wedge:

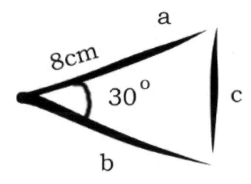

a. 1
b. 2
c. 3
d. 4

5. In the same question, the velocity of block Q, when it reaches a height of 7m above the ground is:
a. 7.33m/s
b. 7.66m/s
c. 7.99m/s
d. Cannot be determined, insufficient data

6. Observe the following figure:

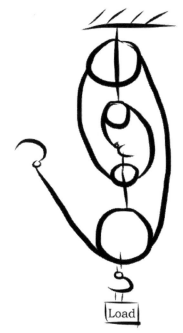

The mechanical advantage (IMA) for this frictionless pulley is:
   a. 3
   b. 4
   c. 5
   d. Insufficient data

7. A body even after applying a certain amount of force, did not move. What can be said about the frictional force acting on the body?
   a. Less than μmg
   b. More than μmg
   c. Equal to mg
   d. Equal to μmg

8. The gravitational force exerted by one object on another at macroscopic level:
   a. Increases with the increase in distance
   b. Decreases with the increase in distance
   c. Remains constant
   d. None of the above

9. The dimensional formula of Gravitational constant is:
   a. ML^2T^{-2}
   b. $M^{-1}L^3T^{-1}$
   c. $M^{-2}L^2T^{-2}$
   d. $M^{-1}L^3T^{-2}$

10. A fighter jet traveling at a speed of 630kmph drops a bomb 8secs before crossing over a target to accurately hit the target. Identify from the figure, the target of the jet:

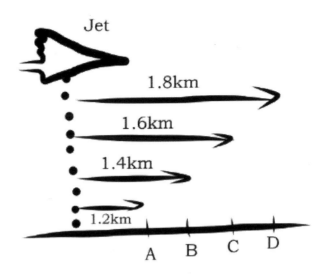

    a. Point A
    b. Point B
    c. Point C
    d. Point D

11. Which of the following is not an equation of uniformly accelerated motion:
    a. $a = v^2 - u^2/2s$
    b. $a = 2(s-ut)/t^2$
    c. $a = 2s-ut/t^2$
    d. $a = v-u/t$

12. Newton's 1st law of motion is based on the Galileo's law of inertia. Which of the following types of inertia satisfy this law:
    a. Inertia of Rest
    b. Inertia of Motion
    c. Inertia of Direction
    d. All of the above

13. Observe the figure below:

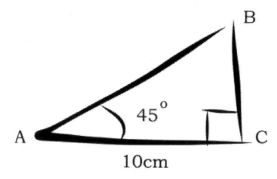

The Mechanical Advantage of the given ramp is:
   a. 1.414
   b. 0.141
   c. 14.14
   d. None of the above

14. Which of the following is not a part of the incline plane family of simple machines:
   a. Wedge
   b. Ramp
   c. Lever
   d. Screw

15. The mechanical advantage of a screw having 6 threads per inch and a radius of 0.1in is:
   a. 3.33
   b. 3.55
   c. 3.77
   d. 3.99

16. Effort is being put on a lever with a speed of 20cm/s at a distance of 2m from the fulcrum. The speed at which the load moves, if it is located at a distance of 50cm from the fulcrum is:
   a. 80 cm/s
   b. 100 cm/s
   c. 120 cm/s
   d. 140 cm/s

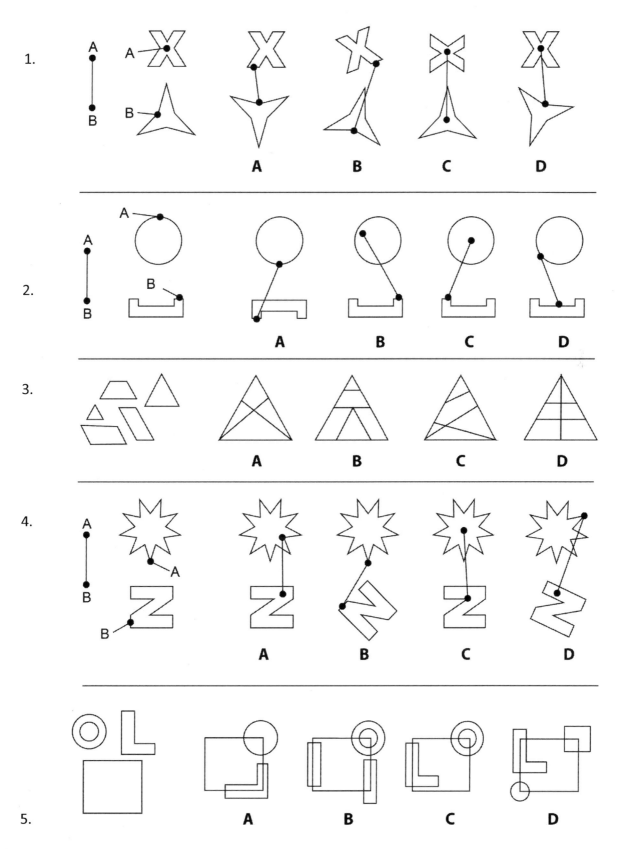

1.
A
B

A
B
A B C D

2.
A
B

A
B
A B C D

3.
A B C D

4.
A
B

A
B
A B C D

5.
A B C D

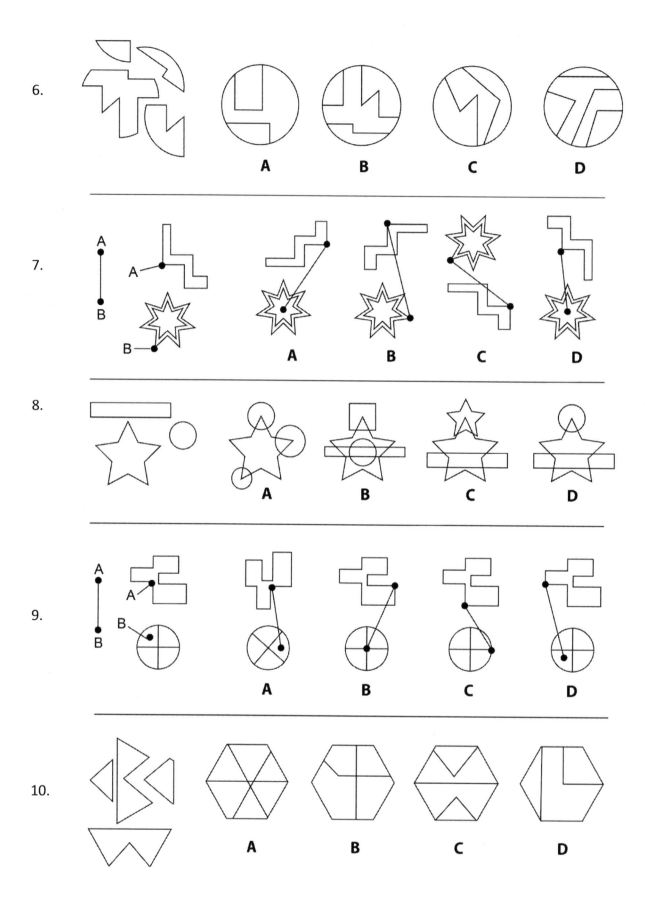

6.

7.

8.

9.

10.

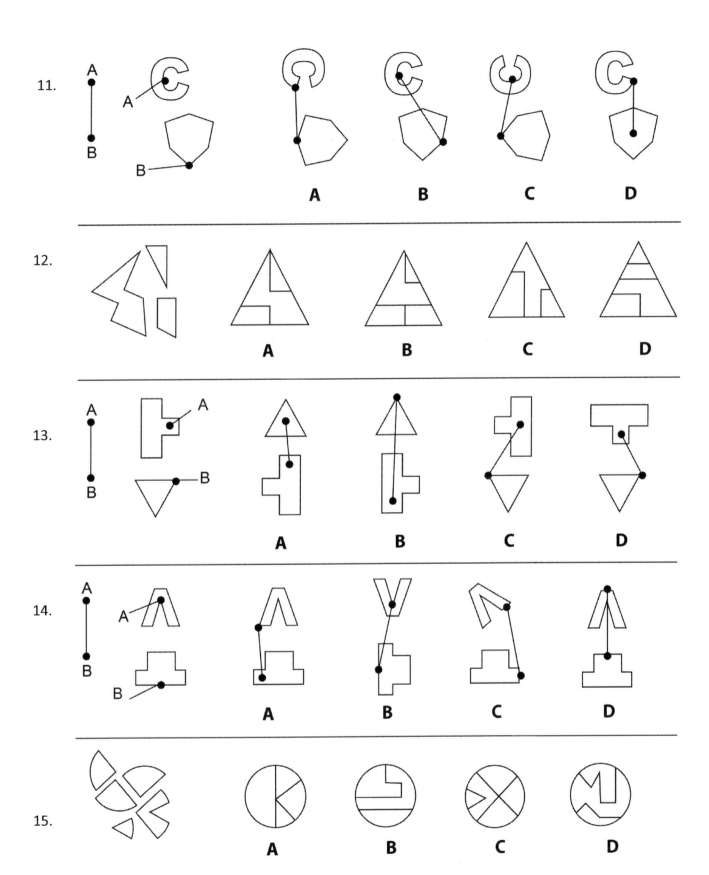

11.

              A   **B**   **C**   **D**

12.

              A   **B**   **C**   **D**

13.

              A   **B**   **C**   **D**

14.

              A   **B**   **C**   **D**

15.

              A   **B**   **C**   **D**

16.

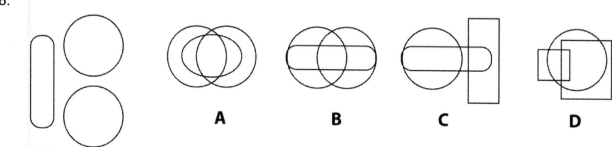

A   B   C   D

Practice Test #3 Answers

GENERAL SCIENCE

1. D.
2. B.
3. B.
4. B.
5. D.
6. A.
7. B.
8. A.
9. C.
10. C.
11. C.
12. B.
13. D.
14. B.
15. C.
16. B.

ARITHMETIC REASONING

1. D.
2. D.
3. D.
4. A.
5. A.
6. B.
7. D.
8. D.
9. A.
10. C.
11. D.
12. A.
13. C.
14. B.
15. D.
16. A.

WORD KNOWLEDGE

1. C.
2. B.
3. D.
4. A.
5. C.
6. C.
7. B.
8. B.
9. A.
10. A.
11. C.
12. A.
13. B.
14. C.
15. D.
16. B.

PARAGRAPH COMPREHENSION

12. B.
13. B.
14. A.
15. C.
16. D.
17. A.
18. B.
19. C.
20. B.
21. D.
22. B.

MATH KNOWLEDGE

1. C.
2. C.
3. D.
4. C.
5. A.
6. A.
7. B.
8. D.
9. C.
10. B.
11. A.
12. D.
13. C.
14. A.
15. A.
16. D.

ELECTRONICS INFORMATION

1. A.
2. B.
3. C.
4. B.
5. C.
6. B.
7. C.
8. A.
9. D.
10. A.
11. C.
12. B.
13. B.
14. C.
15. C.
16. A.

AUTO INFORMATION

1. C.
2. A.
3. A.
4. C.
5. B.
6. B.
7. C.
8. B.
9. B.
10. A.
11. C.

SHOP INFORMATION

1. C.
2. B.
3. D.
4. D.
5. A.
6. D.
7. C.
8. D.
9. D.
10. C.
11. C.

MECHANICAL COMPREHENSION

1. B.
2. A.
3. B.
4. D.
5. B.
6. C.
7. A.
8. B.
9. D.
10. B.
11. C.
12. D.
13. A.
14. C.
15. C.
16. A.

ASSEMBLING OBJECTS

1. D.
2. A.
3. B.
4. B.
5. C.
6. B.
7. B.
8. D.
9. A.
10. C.
11. C.
12. A.
13. D.
14. B.
15. C.
16. B.

GENERAL SCIENCE

17. Which of the following is true regarding deoxyribonucleic acid (DNA. in the human body?
    a. DNA is used as an energy source.
    b. DNA is used as a template for creation of proteins.
    c. DNA is only found in the brain.
    d. DNA is made of sugar.

18. Testes are an organ found in:
    a. Females
    b. Plants
    c. Males
    d. Amoebas

19. How many kingdoms of life are there?
    a. 3
    b. 6
    c. 7
    d. 9

20. Plants absorb carbon dioxide (CO_2) to create sugar for energy. What is the primary byproduct of this process?
    a. Oxygen
    b. Nitrogen
    c. Carbon Monoxide
    d. Carbon

21. What prevents ultraviolet radiation produced by the sun from damaging life on earth?
    a. The ozone layer
    b. Greenhouse gasses
    c. The vacuum between earth and the sun
    d. The water layer

22. Which of the following is *not* present in an animal cell?
    a. Nucleus
    b. Mitochondria
    c. Cytoplasm
    d. Cell Wall

23. Mitosis is the process of cell division to create new cells. What is the process of cell division required to create new sex cells or gametes?
    a. Teloses
    b. Meiosis
    c. Kinesis
    d. Phoresis

24. What are the two main parts of the human body's central nervous system?
    a. The heart and the spinal cord
    b. The brain and the spinal cord
    c. The peripheral nerves and the brain
    d. The spinal cord and the peripheral nerves

25. Which of the following is not an organ system in humans?
    a. The endocrine system
    b. The respiratory system
    c. The exophytic system
    d. The muscular system

26. Humans can turn glucose into ATP, the basic energy molecule in the body. What is a byproduct of this process?
    a. Carbon dioxide
    b. Oxygen
    c. Nitrogen
    d. Phosphorus

27. What is true of elements found in the same group (column) in the periodic table?
    a. They have the same atomic mass
    b. They have the same level of reactivity
    c. They have the same number of protons
    d. The have the same number of valence electrons

28. Compounds that are acidic will be able to lower the pH of a solution, by doing which of the following?
    a. Accepting H+ ions
    b. Releasing H+ ions
    c. Binding with acidic species in solution
    d. Reducing oxidative species in solution

29. Which of the following elements is the most electronegative?
    a. Chlorine
    b. Iron
    c. Magnesium
    d. Silicon

30. According to Newton's first law, F = M x A, how fast will a 10-kilogram object accelerate when pushed with 50 Newtons of force?
    a. $2.5 \ m/s^2$
    b. $5.0 \ m/s^2$
    c. $8.0 \ m/s^2$
    d. $15.0 \ m/s^2$

31. How did mountains on the earth's surface primarily form?
    a. Through the shifting of tectonic plates
    b. Through the impact of meteors
    c. Through gradual erosion
    d. Through accumulation of soil by the wind

32. The age of the Earth is closest to:
    a. 100 million years
    b. 1.2 billion years
    c. 4.5 billion years
    d. 25.0 billion years

ARITHMETIC REASONING

1. Order the following quantities on a number line, from most negative to most positive:
   $2^{-1}, -\frac{4}{3}, (-1)^3, \frac{2}{5}$
   a. $2^{-1}, -\frac{4}{3}, (-1)^3, \frac{2}{5}$
   b. $-\frac{4}{3}, (-1)^3, 2^{-1}, \frac{2}{5}$
   c. $-\frac{4}{3}, \frac{2}{5}, 2^{-1}, (-1)^3$
   d. $-\frac{4}{3}, (-1)^3, \frac{2}{5}, 2^{-1}$

2. $\frac{8}{15}$ is $\frac{1}{6}$ of what number?
   a. $3\frac{1}{15}$
   b. $\frac{15}{48}$
   c. $\frac{4}{45}$
   d. $3\frac{1}{5}$

3. Adam finds a jacket in a store that is marked $\frac{1}{3}$ off. If his student discount gives him an additional $\frac{1}{5}$ off the original price, by what fraction is the jacket discounted in total?
   a. $\frac{1}{15}$
   b. $\frac{6}{15}$
   c. $\frac{7}{15}$
   d. $\frac{8}{15}$

4. $0.003856 =$
   a. 3856×10^{-6}
   b. 385.6×10^{-5}
   c. 3.856×10^{-3}
   d. 3.856×10^3

5. Simplify: $[56 \div (2 \times 2^2)] - 9 \div 3$
   a. 4
   b. -0.667
   c. 34.33
   d. 109

6. Becky is filling her rectangular swimming pool for the summer. The pool is 10 meters long, 6 meters wide, and 1.5 meters deep. How much water will she need to fill the pool?
    a. 90 meters
    b. 90 m^2
    c. 90 m^3
    d. 90 m^4

7. Patrick is coming home from vacation to Costa Rica and wants to fill one of his suitcases with bags of Costa Rican coffee. The weight limit for his suitcase is 22 kilograms, and the suitcase itself weighs 3.2 kilograms. If each bag of coffee weighs 800 grams, how many bags can he bring in his suitcase without going over the limit?
    a. 27
    b. 23
    c. 4
    d. 2

8. If *m* represents a car's average mileage in miles per gallon, *p* represents the price of gas in dollars per gallon, and *d* represents a distance in miles, which of the following algebraic equations represents the cost (*c*) of gas per mile?
    a. $c = \dfrac{dp}{m}$
    b. $c = \dfrac{p}{m}$
    c. $c = \dfrac{mp}{d}$
    d. $c = \dfrac{m}{p}$

9. Find the next term in the following sequence: $5, 12, 19, 26, \ldots$
    a. 35
    b. 37
    c. 33
    d. 34

10. Suppose Mark can mow the entire lawn in 47 minutes, and Mark's dad can mow the entire lawn in 53 minutes. If Mark and his dad work together (each with their own lawnmowers), how long will it take them to mow the entire lawn?
    a. 15.6 minutes
    b. 24.9 minutes
    c. 26.5 minutes
    d. 50 minutes

11. The kinetic energy, K, of an object is given in terms of its mass, m, and velocity, v, as shown in the equation $K = \frac{1}{2}mv^2$. Object A and object B have the same mass. If object A is moving at half the velocity of object B, the kinetic energy of object A is what fraction of the kinetic energy of object B?

   a. $\frac{1}{2}$

   b. $\frac{1}{4}$

   c. $\frac{1}{16}$

   d. $\frac{1}{64}$

12. Stephanie eats 0.625 of her pizza. If her pizza was cut into 8 slices, how many slices has she eaten?

   a. 3
   b. 4
   c. 5
   d. 6

13. Gym A offers a monthly membership for 80% of the cost at Gym B; the cost at Gym B is 115% the cost of Gym C. What percentage of the cost at Gym C does Gym A charge?

   a. 35%
   b. 97%
   c. 70%
   d. 92%

14. Simplify: 54.48 ÷ 0.6

   a. 0.908
   b. 9.08
   c. 90.8
   d. 908

15. John and Jake are working at a car wash. It takes John 1 hour to wash 3 cars; Jake can wash 3 cars in 45 minutes. If they work together, how many cars can they wash in 1 hour?

   a. 6 cars
   b. 7 cars
   c. 9 cars
   d. 12 cars

16. Melissa is ordering fencing to enclose a square area of 5625 square feet. How many feet of fencing does she need?
    a. 75 feet
    b. 150 feet
    c. 300 feet
    d. 5,625 feet

WORD KNOWLEDGE

1. The course was <u>required.</u>
   a. Mandatory
   b. Voluntary
   c. Managed
   d. Volatile

2. Stalwart most closely means:
   a. Weak
   b. Ill
   c. Brave
   d. Stubborn

3. His responses and personality were <u>brusque</u>.
   a. Cheerful
   b. Slow
   c. Curt
   d. Angry

4. Subordinate most nearly means:
   a. Lower
   b. Higher
   c. Larger
   d. Smaller

5. The test caused him to feel <u>apprehensive</u>.
   a. Nervous
   b. Terrified
   c. Excited
   d. Elated

6. Proscribe most closely means:
   a. Prohibit
   b. Prescribe
   c. Require
   d. Write

7. Infallible most nearly means:
    a. Flawed
    b. Broken
    c. Inaccurate
    d. Flawless

8. He was <u>meticulous</u> about his appearance in uniform.
    a. Thorough
    b. Conscientious
    c. Lackadaisical
    d. Pretentious

9. She was <u>deferential</u> to her commanding officers.
    a. Disrespectful
    b. Respectful
    c. Rude
    d. Pleasant

10. Comply most nearly means:
    a. Hurry
    b. Follow
    c. Ignore
    d. Obey

11. Deploy most nearly means:
    a. Post
    b. Fight
    c. Ship
    d. Return

12. Inept most closely means:
    a. Clumsy
    b. Skilled
    c. Conscientious
    d. Incompetent

13. He was a _conscientious_ worker.
   a. Careless
   b. Sloppy
   c. Careful
   d. Slow

14. Malevolent most closely means:
   a. Bad
   b. Good
   c. Slow
   d. Fast

15. Treacherous most nearly means:
   a. Illegal
   b. Dangerous
   c. Unhealthy
   d. Immoral

16. He was _irate_ when his instructions were not followed to the letter.
   a. Irritated
   b. Frustrated
   c. Enraged
   d. Calm

PARAGRAPH COMPREHENSION

1. Between April 1860 and October 1861 **The Pony Express** delivered mail, news, and other forms of communication from Missouri across the Great Plains, through the Rocky Mountains, through the desert lands of Nevada to California, using only man and horse power. The Pony Express closed in October of 1861; just two days after the transcontinental telegraph reached Salt Lake City, therefore, connecting Omaha, and Nebraska to California. Other telegraph lines connect many other cities along the Pony Express Route.

    Why did the Pony Express close?
    a. The Civil War stopped them from running their business.
    b. Another company was faster and took over the business.
    c. The Pony Express riders were unable to pass through the Rocky Mountains in the winter months.
    d. With the transcontinental telegraph connecting so many cities along the route, the Pony Express became redundant.

2. Between 1914 and 1935, George Herman "Babe" Ruth Jr. was known as "the Bambino" to baseball fans. Over his 22 seasons, he only played for three teams (Boston Red Sox, New York Yankees, and Boston Braves) and was known most for his hitting skills and RBI's statistics. Due mostly to Babe Ruth's hitting ability baseball changed during the 1920's from a fast-playing game with lower scores to one of higher scores and a slower pace.

    How did "The Bambino's" hitting skills and RBI's statistics affect the way baseball was played?
    a. He hit so many batters in that the game went faster.
    b. The innings lasted longer with so many batters scoring runs.
    c. They had to stop the game because every time Babe Ruth hit a home run fans mobbed him.
    d. The Regulations changed which caused the game to last longer.

3. **Kraft Macaroni and Cheese** goes by many names. In Canada, it is called Kraft Dinner and in the United Kingdom it is known as Cheesy Pasta. No matter what name it is called by, this pasta dish has been a staple of the typical North American diet since its beginning in 1937. James Lewis Kraft, a Canadian living in Chicago struck gold by introducing this product during WWII, when more and more women were working outside of the home, milk and other dairy foods were rationed and hearty "meatless" meals were relied upon.

   Why has this product continued to be a staple in our diet over 75 years after it was introduced to Americans?
   a. Most Americans love pasta and cheese.
   b. It is still the cheapest pasta on the market.
   c. The same factors that made its introduction so popular still exist today.
   d. It is still popular today because of brilliant marketing strategies.

4. The **Declaration of Independence** was unanimously voted on July 2 and adopted by the *Continental Congress* on July 4, 1776; declaring considered themselves no longer one of Britain's colonies. The official announcement was also made on July 4th to the people of the original thirteen American "states" that made up the new country known as the United States of America.

   Why is Independence Day celebrated on July 4th and not July 2nd when the unanimous vote occurred?
   a. Since July 4th was the first weekday that the American people heard the announcement of the **Declaration of Independence**, that is the day that people counted as the first day as an independent country.
   b. Officially, until the **Declaration of independence** was adopted by the *Continental Congress* and announced to the people of the thirteen colonies, it was not considered legally binding.
   c. Legally the Declaration of Independence should be observed on July 2; the people of the U.S.A. are wrong.
   d. The politicians involved in the original signing of the **Declaration of Independence** didn't want their new country's birthday to be the day after Canada celebrates the date they became a country independent of the British Empire.

5. The Statue of Liberty was a gift from the people of France and was dedicated on October 28, 1886. She is an iconic symbol of patriotism to the people of the United States of America and even has the date of the American Declaration of Independence, July 4, 1776, chiseled on the tablet she is holding. Displayed on Liberty Island, this statue is a beacon of hope and freedom to immigrants from around the world.

   Why is the Statue of Liberty a symbol of hope and freedom to immigrants from around the world?
   a. The Statue of Liberty is the very first site that any immigrant traveling by boat sees when entering the New York Harbor. She is the epitome of everything the United States of America stands for, "Life, Liberty, and the pursuit of Happiness."
   b. The Statue of Liberty has been the only symbol of the United States that has been used in films and other forms of media that people in other countries have seen and, therefore, associates it with the country.
   c. The Statue of Liberty was a sign of peace sent from France after they lost the Great War to the United States. It was a sign of freedom because the U.S.A did not conquer their country when they won the war and a sign of hope that peace will reign between the two countries.
   d. Immigrants know that once they have passed the Statue of Liberty, under no circumstances will they be forced to return to their home country and lose the freedom of living in the United States of America.

6. Mickey Mouse is the official mascot of The Walt Disney Company and was first created in 1928 by Walt Disney and Ub Iwerks as a roguish antihero. Since his first appearance in test screening of Plane Crazy, Mickey Mouse has appeared in over 130 films, comic strips, comic books, video games, television series, and is now a lovable, friendly character that can be seen at all of the Disney Theme Parks.

   Why has Mickey's character changed from antihero to fun-loving and adventurous over the last 80 years or so?
      a. Mickey Mouse scared children when he was first introduced as an impish antihero and Walt Disney was forced to change his characteristics or create another character to be the official mascot.
      b. Although Mickey Mouse was first created as an adult character, Walt Disney realized that more and more children were watching the movies, therefore, he altered his image to be more "child-like" so that his younger audience could identify with him.
      c. As Mickey Mouse's popularity grew, and more characters were developed to be his friends, such as Minnie Mouse, Pluto, and Donald Duck, it was only natural that his personality changed into a friendlier, fun-loving character.
      d. Walt Disney received thousands of letters from parents complaining that their children were misbehaving and acting out the behaviors of the mischievous mouse featured in the Disney films and comics. Walt Disney was pressured by the public to change Mickey Mouse's characteristics, or America's parents would have boycotted the entire Disney brand.

7. Nelson Mandela, Steve Biko, Desmond Tutu, Denis Goldberg, and Harry Schwarz are all activists that fought against the system of apartheid in countries such as South Africa during the 1980's and 1990's.

    What is the meaning of the word "Apartheid"?
    a. Apartheid is a system of segregation based on a person's race that was law in South Africa between 1948 and 1994.
    b. Apartheid is a system by which people in South Africa are dictated where they are allowed to live and who they can marry based on how much wealth their family has accrued.
    c. Apartheid is the name given to the trade embargo placed on the country of South Africa by the United States of America between 1950's and 1990's.
    d. Apartheid is a system of classification South Africa, based on the race of your grandparents; therefore, every second generation is able to apply for a change in classification based on inter-racial changes in the family tree.

8. The "Anti-Fascist Protection Rampart" was the official name given to the Berlin Wall. This wall was a large concrete wall with guard towers that completely blocked West Berlin from both East Germany and East Berlin. It was claimed by the German Democratic Republic (GDR), the political party in power after the end of WWII in Eastern Germany, that this wall was built to protect the people from the fascist interests attempting to prevent East Berliners from building a socialist state which was their idea of utopia. Between the years of 1961 and 1989 it is estimated that 5000 people attempted to escape over the wall resulting in over 100 deaths.

    What is implied by the fact that so many people "attempted to escape" over the Berlin Wall?
    a. It is implied that many Western Germans wanted to live in Eastern Germany and live in their utopia county.
    b. It is implied that Eastern Germany was very "fore-thinking" in their policies for national security although, a little over-the-top compared to today's standards.
    c. Although the political party believed in "protecting" the people of East Germany, many East German's were not in agreement with the "utopia" world that was developed but were not free to just leave.
    d. East Germans had to pay a very high tax in order to be able to move out of the area, so many people tried to leave without having to pay so much money to the government.

9. A tropical cyclone is a storm system that rotates very quickly and is pigeonholed by strong winds, heavy rain, and a low-pressure center. Some names that a tropical cyclone is referred to as include: typhoon, hurricane, and tropical depression.

In this paragraph, what does the word "pigeonholed" means?
   a. A small compartment that is part of a set on a desk or wall unit into which things are placed.
   b. A small hole in a tree where birds build a nest.
   c. A hole in a piece of wood that is roughly the size of a pigeon.
   d. A broad category or label given to someone or something.

10. Historically, archeologists have identified many dinosaurs that are omnivores. This means that eat both plants and meat. Other dinosaurs are only plant-eaters or meat-eaters; they are referred to as herbivores and carnivores, respectively.

What is the main idea in this paragraph?
   a. The main idea is that there were herbivore, carnivore, and omnivore dinosaurs on this planet thousands of years ago.
   b. The main idea of this paragraph is that archeologists have identified different types of dinosaurs.
   c. Herbivores were dinosaurs that ate only a diet of plants; this is the main idea of the paragraph.
   d. The main idea of this paragraph is that carnivores were dinosaurs that only ate other animals.

11. The RMS Titanic, although built in Belfast, Ireland, was a British passenger ship that collided with an iceberg in the North Atlantic on April 15, 1912, and sank to the bottom of the ocean. More than 1,500 souls died in what is considered one of the deadliest maritime disasters outside of war.

The ocean liner only had enough lifeboats for just over half of the number of people on board. In this paragraph, what does RMS stand for?
   a. Royal Majesty's Service
   b. Royal Mail Ship
   c. Royal Majesty's Ship
   d. Royal Mail Steamer

MATH KNOWLEDGE

1. $\frac{4}{5} \div \frac{6}{7} \times \frac{1}{2} + \frac{3}{2}$

    a. $\frac{56}{30}$

    b. $\frac{57}{30}$

    c. $\frac{58}{30}$

    d. $\frac{59}{30}$

2. What will be the value of $x^3+6x^2+12x+16$ when $x = -2$?

    a. 8

    b. 24

    c. 48

    d. 72

3. ABCD is a rectangle and inside it ABE is an Equilateral Triangle. What will be the angle <CEA represented by x in the figure?

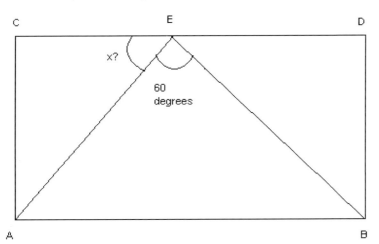

    a. 45°

    b. 50°

    c. 60°

    d. 55°

4. Which of the following numbers will satisfy this equation $\frac{n(n+1)(n+2)}{n(n+4)} = 2$

    a. 1
    b. 2
    c. 3
    d. 4

5. If $6x^2+7y = 45$ is an equation. What will be the value of y if x=2??

    a. 4
    b. 1
    c. 2
    d. 3

6. The figure shows a right-angled triangle with side AC = 5m. Find the length of side AB

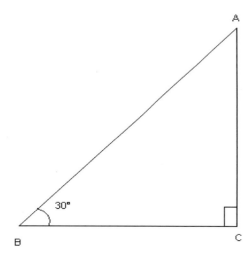

    a. 7
    b. 8
    c. 9
    d. 10

7. If z= $\frac{6y^2}{3x}$. What will be the value of z for y = 3x and x=2?

    a. 36
    b. 30
    c. 32
    d. 40

8. If we divide the first number by the second number, we get 3, and the sum of both numbers is 16. What will be the numbers?

    a. 15, 5
    b. 12, 4
    c. 9, 3
    d. 18, 6

9. What will be the point of intersection of two lines 3x+2y-8=0 & 4x+7y-15=0??

    a. (1, 2)
    b. (2, 1)
    c. (1, 3)
    d. these are non-intersecting lines.

10. How many prime numbers are less than 29?

    a. 7
    b. 8
    c. 9
    d. 10

11. 5500000 is not equal to which of the following

    a. 5.50×10^6
    b. 550×10^4
    c. 55×10^6
    d. 0.55×10^7

12. What is the correct order if the following fractions are placed in order from top to bottom $\frac{1}{3}, \frac{1}{2}, \frac{3}{4}, \frac{5}{6}$??

    a. $\frac{1}{2}, \frac{5}{6}, \frac{3}{4}, \frac{1}{3}$
    b. $\frac{5}{6}, \frac{1}{2}, \frac{1}{3}, \frac{3}{4}$
    c. $\frac{3}{4}, \frac{1}{3}, \frac{1}{2}, \frac{5}{6}$
    d. $\frac{5}{6}, \frac{3}{4}, \frac{1}{2}, \frac{1}{3}$

13. $-(-5)^3 \div (-5)^2 = $ ....

    a. -125
    b. 25
    c. 125
    d. -25

14. $\left(\dfrac{2a^{10}b^6}{3}\right) \div \left(\dfrac{15a^2b}{2\,a^{-3}}\right)^{-1} = \ldots\ldots$

     a. $5a^9\,b^7$

     b. $5a^{15}\,b^5$

     c. $5a^{12}\,b^7$

     d. $5a^{15}\,b^7$

15. If the sum of the digits of a number is 11 and product of its digits is 16 and the difference of the tenth unit digit from hundredth unit digit is 6. What is the number?

     a. 821

     b. 812

     c. 218

     d. 128

16. If x>y, y<z, x>z, such that product of x, y and z is 72. What will be the numbers?

     a. x=6, y=4, z=3

     b. x=4, y=6, z=3

     c. x=3, y=4, z=6

     d. x=6, y=3, z=4

14. $\left(\dfrac{2a^{10}b^6}{3}\right) \div \left(\dfrac{15a^2b}{2\,a^{-3}}\right)^{-1} = \ldots\ldots$

ELECTRONICS INFORMATION

1. The minimum amount of energy required to disclose an electron from a covalent bond is called which of the following?
   a. Transition Energy
   b. Bandgap Energy
   c. Thermal Energy
   d. Potential Energy

2. An intrinsic semi-conductor is a semi-conductor in which:
   a. No significant dopant species are present, and it is a pure semi-conductor.
   b. A doping agent has been added to change its properties.
   c. The concentrations of electrons and holes change due to doping
   d. The resistivity of the semi-conductor can change by adding impurities

3. Which of the following statements is correct regarding the flow of current?
   a. The current flows from low potential to high potential.
   b. The current flows in the opposite direction of electric field.
   c. The current flows from high potential to low potential.
   d. The current flow does not depend on the potential difference.

4. The capacitor blocks Direct Current (D.C.).Hence, it is also known as:
   a. Blocking Capacitor
   b. Switched Capacitor
   c. Coupling Capacitor
   d. Both options A and C

5. According to Ohm's Law, what will happen to the resistance if the current increases?
   a. Resistance will increase
   b. Resistance will decrease
   c. Resistance will remain same
   d. Resistance will become zero

6. The resistance of a wire is R. What will be the resistance if the length of the wire becomes double, and the cross-sectional areas become half?
   a. (1/4)R
   b. R
   c. 2R
   d. 4R

7. What is the equivalent capacitance of four capacitors connected in parallel if the value of each capacitor is 4F?
   a. 1F
   b. 10F
   c. 16F
   d. 20F

8. What are two terminals of a diode?
   a. Collector, Cathode
   b. Anode, Cathode
   c. Anode, Emitter
   d. Emitter, Collector

9. The diode which is designed to go through avalanche breakdown at a specified reverse bias voltage is called:
   a. Light-emitting diode
   b. Avalanche Diode
   c. Varactor Diode
   d. Switching Diode

10. Which one of the following is not a region of operation of a diode?
    a. Forward-bias Region
    b. Breakdown Region
    c. Saturation Region
    d. Reverse-bias Region

11. BJT stands for which of the following?
    a. Biased Junction Transistor
    b. Bisection Junction Transistor
    c. Bidirectional Junction Transistor
    d. Bipolar Junction Transistor

12. What is the function of an inductor?
    a. Storing Current
    b. Controlling Current
    c. Acting as a non-passive device
    d. Creating potential difference

13. What is the function of an inverter?
    a. It converts AC to DC
    b. It steps up AC
    c. It converts DC to AC
    d. It steps up DC

14. What is the function of a transformer?
    a. It transforms voltage.
    b. It transforms current.
    c. It transforms power.
    d. It transforms both voltage and current.

15. Which one of the following is a step-down DC to DC converter?
    a. Boost Converter
    b. Buck Converter
    c. Transformer
    d. Inverter

16. Power factor is represented by which of the following?
    a. cos θ
    b. sin θ
    c. tan θ
    d. cot θ

AUTO INFORMATION

1. Which of the following ignition systems has contact points?
    a. Distributorless Ignition
    b. Direct Ignition
    c. Capacitor Discharge Ignition
    d. None of the above

2. The catalytic converter is a component of which automotive system?
    a. Emission Control System
    b. Drive Train
    c. Safety System
    d. Cooling System

3. What can be the side effects of worn piston rings?
    a. Increased oil consumption
    b. White or gray smoke
    c. Low power
    d. All of the above

4. How many times does the crankshaft rotate during a complete cycle of a four-stroke engine?
    a. 1
    b. 2
    c. 3
    d. 4

5. What is the most common type of automotive engine?
    a. Rotary
    b. Four Cycle
    c. Two Cycle
    d. External Combustion

6. If an engine is being supplied with too much fuel, the air-fuel mixture is said to be:
    a. Rich
    b. Lean
    c. Stoichiometric
    d. High Octane

7. What gauge shows the speed of an engine in rpm?
   a. Speedometer
   b. Tripometer
   c. Tachometer
   d. Fuel Gauge

8. Most modern automotive brake systems are activated:
   a. Mechanically
   b. Electronically
   c. Hydraulically
   d. Pneumatically

9. How is fuel mixed into the airstream entering a carbureted engine?
   a. Low pressure in the venturi of the carburetor
   b. Injectors controlled by the Power Control Module (PCM)
   c. High pressure in the fuel line created by the fuel pump
   d. Both a and c

10. In a gasoline engine, an air-fuel mixture of 11:1 would be considered:
    a. Rich
    b. Lean
    c. Stoichiometric
    d. None of the above

11. A car's radiator transfers heat from the _____ to the air.
    a. Engine oil
    b. Distributor
    c. Coolant
    d. Brake Fluid

SHOP INFORMATION

1. Which tool can be used to measure an angle?
    a. Compass
    b. Protractor
    c. Dial indicator
    d. Calipers

2. Which of the following cuts with a pulling motion?
    a. Backsaw
    b. File
    c. Pull saw
    d. Ripsaw

3. Which of these is not a common type of file?
    a. Flat
    b. Half-round
    c. Hexagon
    d. Triangle

4. What tool would be used to tighten a bolt to 20 ft-lb?
    a. Torque wrench
    b. Breaker bar
    c. Pipe wrench
    d. Box wrench

5. Which tool is used to remove a small strip from wood?
    a. File
    b. Ripsaw
    c. Plane
    d. Chisel

6. Which of these saws creates the widest kerf?
    a. Crosscut saw
    b. Jigsaw
    c. Ripsaw
    d. Hacksaw

7. What is the pitch of an M10 X 1.25 X 40 bolt?
    a. 10 mm
    b. 1.25 tpi
    c. 40 tpi
    d. 1.25 mm

8. Which of the following should be used to cut wood along the grain?
   a. Crosscut saw
   b. Ripsaw
   c. Backsaw
   d. Knife

9. Which fractional screw has the finest thread?
   a. 1/4 – 20 X 3/4
   b. 10 – 32 X 1
   c. 7/16 – 20 X 2
   d. 1/2 – 24 X 3

10. Which of these tools is considered a fastening tool?
    a. Stapler
    b. Screwdriver
    c. Plier
    d. All of the above

11. Which of the following is a thread type?
    a. Unified National Coarse
    b. Unified National Wide Thread
    c. Unified National Fine
    d. Both a and c

MECHANICAL COMPREHENSION

1. Calculate the amount of work done in moving a mass of 10kg at rest with a force of 5N in 8 seconds with no repulsive forces in action?
    a. 80J
    b. 100J
    c. 120J
    d. 60J

2. Consider 3 equal masses at arbitrary points A, B & C in space and let D be a point on the surface of the earth (as shown in the figure).

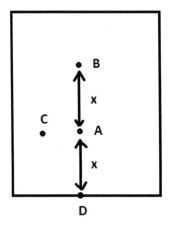

Then,
    i.   The mass at point B has the maximum potential energy
    ii. Masses at points A & C have equal P.E. but less than that of the mass at point D
    iii. The mass at point D, if lifted to a height 2x, will possess P.E. equal to P.E(B.
    a. Statements (i), (ii) & (iii) are true
    b. Only statements (i) & (iii) are true
    c. None of them is true
    d. Only statements (i) is true

3. The disc in the figure is set to roll with angular velocity omega.

m

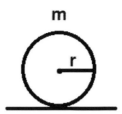

Total energy of the ball is:
   a. $^1/_2 mr^2 w^2$
   b. $^3/_4 mrw^2$
   c. $^1/_2 mrw^2$
   d. $^3/_4 mr^2 w^2$

4. Consider the following table:

S.No.	Length (cm)	Breadth (cm)
Wedge 1	5	2
Wedge 2	7	3
Wedge 3	4	6
Wedge 4	9	4

Which of the above wedges will provide maximum Mechanical Advantage?
   a. Wedge 1
   b. Wedge 2
   c. Wedge 3
   d. Wedge 4

5. A block P of mass 100kg is tied to one end of a rope on a frictionless pulley to lift another block Q with mass 40kg. What is the amount of acceleration produced in the rope during the lifting action?

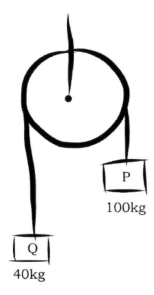

    a. 2.4m/s^2
    b. 3.3m/s^2
    c. 4.2m/s^2
    d. 5.1m/s^2

6. In the above problem, the value of acceleration for block P & Q are:
    a. Negative & Positive respectively
    b. Positive & Negative respectively
    c. Both Negative
    d. Both Positive

7. A train of mass 100 tons is traveling with a uniform velocity of 108kmph. The driver is informed about a broken bridge 250m away from his present location. He immediately applies the brakes. If the coefficient of friction between the train and the rails is 0.2, what is the uniform deceleration achieved by the train after the brakes were applied?
    a. 1.88m/s^2
    b. 1.92m/s^2
    c. 1.96m/s^2
    d. 2.00m/s^2

8. In the above problem, was the driver able to prevent the accident?
    a. Yes
    b. No
    c. Can't be determined
    d. None of the above

9. Acceleration of a moving body can be determined by:
    a. Slope of velocity-time graph
    b. Area under velocity time graph
    c. Slope of distance-time graph
    d. Area under distance-time graph

10. Ratio of the distance traveled by a free falling body in the 1st 3 seconds is:
    a. 1:4:8
    b. 1:2:3
    c. 1:7:11
    d. 1:4:9

11. Which type of simple machine is used in each case?
    • Woodcutter using an ax
    • Lady withdrawing water from well
    • Children playing on see-saw
    • A mechanic working with nuts and bolts
    a. Screw, Wedge, Pulley, Lever
    b. Wedge, Pulley, Lever, Screw
    c. Pulley, Lever, Screw, Wedge
    d. Lever, Screw, Wedge, Pulley

12. Which of the following statements is true:
    a. IMA is always > AMA
    b. IMA is always < AMA
    c. IMA is always = AMA
    d. None of the above

13. Which of the following statements is true:
    i. F_E is in the middle of the 3rd class lever
    ii. Fulcrum is in the middle of the 1st class lever
    iii. F_R is in the middle of the 2nd class lever
    a. Only statement (i) & (ii) are correct
    b. All statements are correct
    c. Only statement (ii) is correct
    d. None of the statements is correct

14. Consider the following statements:
   i.   Only order 1 and order 2 levers multiply force
   ii. Mechanical Advantage of 3rd order lever is always < 1
   a. Statement (i) is true, but statement (ii) is false
   b. Statement (i) is false, but statement (ii) is true
   c. Both statements are true, but statement (ii) is not the correct explanation of statement (i)
   d. Both statements are true & statement (ii) is the correct explanation of statement (i)

15. In wrestling matches, soft ground is provided instead of hard ground because:
   a. During fall, frictional force can cause burns to wrestler
   b. Hitting ground is an impulsive force
   c. Soft ground provides better recoil
   d. None of the above

16. A 100kg stone and a bird feather are allowed to free fall in the vacuum from a height of 50m. The time taken by 100kg stone to reach ground is:
   a. Less than the time taken by the feather
   b. Greater than the time taken by the feather
   c. Equal to the time taken by the feather
   d. Infinite as there is no force exerted because the medium is vacuum

ASSEMBLING OBJECTS

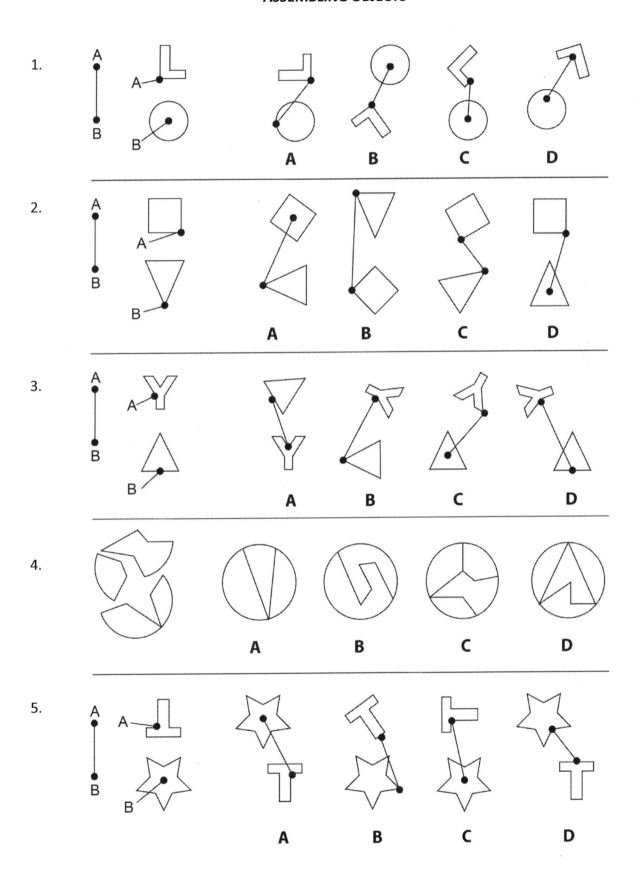

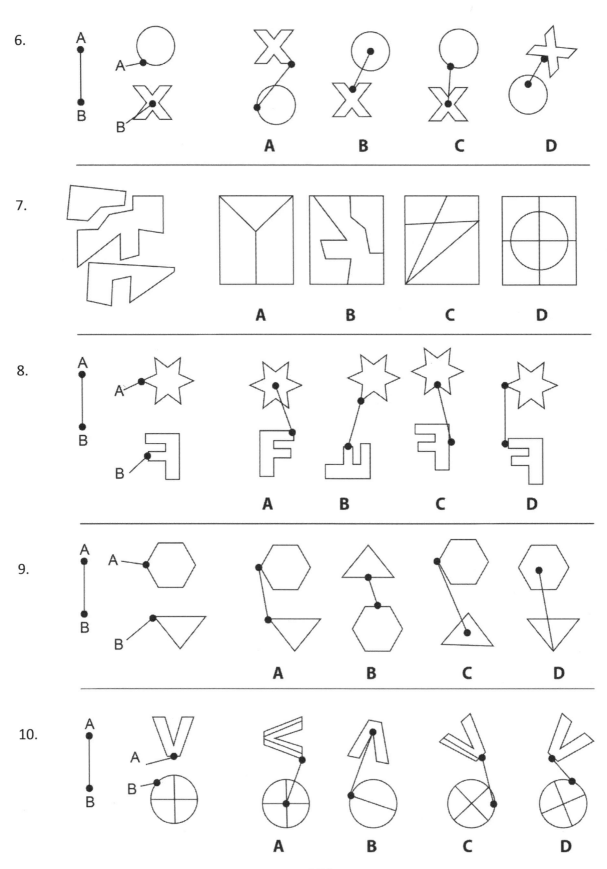

6.

7.

8.

9.

10.

194

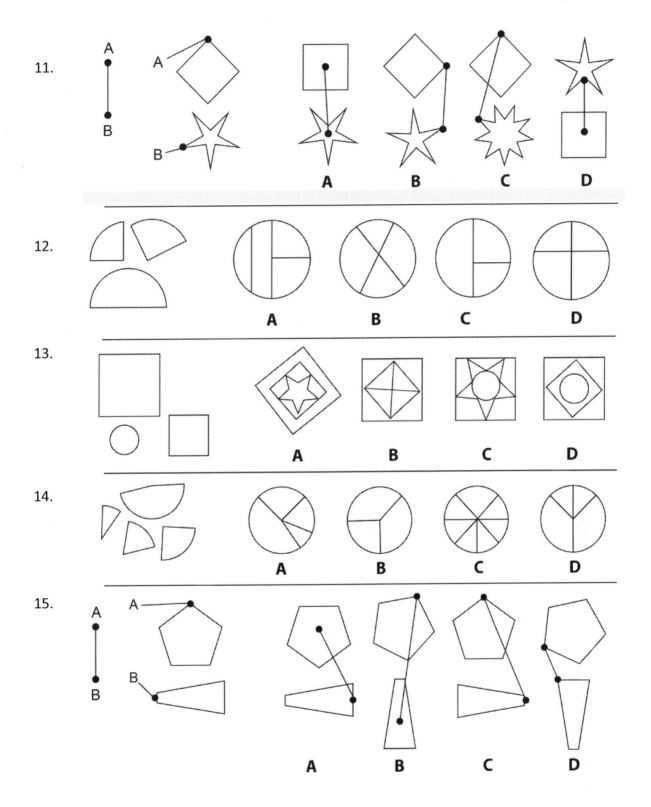

11.

12.

13.

14.

15.

195

16.

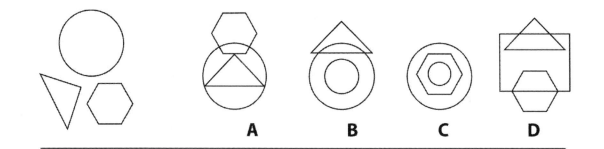

A   B   C   D

GENERAL SCIENCE

1. B.
2. C.
3. B.
4. A.
5. A.
6. D.
7. B.
8. B.
9. C.
10. A.
11. D.
12. B.
13. A.
14. B.
15. A.
16. C.

ARITHMETIC REASONING

1. B.
2. C.
3. B.
4. D.
5. D.
6. B.
7. C.
8. B.
9. A.
10. A.
11. A.
12. D.
13. D.
14. A.
15. D.
16. D.

WORD KNOWLEDGE

1. A.
2. C.
3. C.
4. A.
5. A.
6. A.
7. D.
8. B.
9. B.
10. D.
11. A.
12. A.
13. C.
14. A.
15. B.
16. C.

PARAGRAPH COMPREHENSION

1. D.
2. B.
3. C.
4. B.
5. A.
6. C.
7. A.
8. C.
9. A.
10. B.
11. C.

MATH KNOWLEDGE

1. D.
2. A.
3. C.
4. B.
5. D.
6. D.
7. A.
8. B.
9. B.
10. C.
11. C.
12. D.
13. B.
14. D.
15. A.
16. D.

ELECTRONICS INFORMATION

1. B.
2. A.
3. C.
4. D.
5. B.
6. D.
7. C.
8. B.
9. B.
10. C.
11. D.
12. A.
13. C.
14. D.
15. B.
16. A.

AUTO INFORMATION

1. D.
2. A.
3. D.
4. B.
5. B.
6. A.
7. C.
8. C.
9. D.
10. A.
11. C.

SHOP INFORMATION

1. B.
2. C.
3. C.
4. A.
5. C.
6. A.
7. D.
8. B.
9. B.
10. D.
11. D.

MECHANICAL COMPREHENSION

1. A.
2. B.
3. D.
4. A.
5. C.
6. A.
7. C.
8. A.
9. A.
10. D.
11. B.
12. A.
13. B.
14. D.
15. B.
16. C.

ASSEMBLING OBJECTS

1. B.
2. C.
3. D.
4. C.
5. A.
6. C.
7. B.
8. B.
9. A.
10. D.
11. B.
12. C.
13. D.
14. A.
15. C.
16. A.

Made in the USA
San Bernardino, CA
07 July 2018

81463748R00115